The Development of Nomadism in Ancient Northeast Africa

The Development of
NOMADISM
in Ancient
Northeast Africa

KARIM SADR

upp

University of Pennsylvania Press
Philadelphia

Library of Congress Cataloging-in-Publication Data
Sadr, Karim.
    The development of nomadism in ancient northeast Africa / Karim
Sadr.
      p.   cm.
    Includes bibliographical references and index.
    ISBN 0-8122-3066-3
      1. Nomads—Africa, Northeast.   2. Africa, Northeast—Antiquities.
    3. Africa, Northeast—Economic conditions.   I. Title.
    GN650.S23   1991
    305.9′0693—dc20   91-14688
                                                                 CIP

For my Parents
DR. DJAVAD
and
IRMGARD SADR

Contents

Figures and Tables

Tables

Acknowledgments

This book is a revised version of my dissertation, which was in part based on archaeological fieldwork in the Sudan carried out under the auspices of two separate projects: the Butana Archaeological Project (BAP), a joint effort by Southern Methodist University and the University of Khartoum, funded by the U.S. National Science Foundation (grant no. BNS 8102649); and the University of Naples Istituto Universitario Orientale Italian Archaeological Mission in Sudan, Kassala (IAMSK), funded by the Italian Ministry of Education (research funds 40%), the Italian Ministry of Foreign Affairs, and the Italian National Research Council. I am greatly indebted to Professor Anthony E. Marks, director of the BAP, for selecting me as his project surveyor. The generosity of Dr. Rodolfo Fattovich, the director of the IAMSK, in allowing me to survey for his project during the 1982 and 1984 seasons, ensured the scale of spatial coverage without which the present study would have been meaningless.

Along with my gratitude to the directors of these projects, many thanks are due to the other members of the teams. On the BAP side, I am particularly grateful to Dr. Abbas Mohammed-Ali and Dr. Yousef El-Amin, as well as to a number of the archaeology students from the University of Khartoum who accompanied the project in the field. Thanks are also due to Dr. T.R. Hays, Lewis McNaughten, Dr. Achilles Gautier, and my then fellow students Stephen M'Butu and Joris Peters.

On the IAMSK side, I am grateful to Dr. Rodolfo Fattovich and Dr. Marcello Piperno, Christina Damiani, Adele D'Alessandro, Mauro Coltorti, and Bruno Castielli for some of the most enjoyable field seasons I have experienced. Many thanks also to my friend Shukri, whose tireless efforts, as both field worker and guide, contributed much to the work in Kassala.

For their assistance and friendship, I am deeply grateful to the staff and faculty of the Department of Archaeology, University of Khartoum, and to the inspectors of the Directorate General for Antiquities and National Museums of the Sudan. A very special note of thanks to Patrice Lenoble of the French Archaeological Research Unit, for his hospitality in Khartoum and inspiring professionalism in the field.

Away from the field, many have been helpful in bringing this book to publication. In particular I would like to thank Professor Anthony E. Marks for the constant encouragement and unflinching support he gave my research. In addition to Professor Marks, Dr. Rodolfo Fattovich, Professor C. Garth Sampson, and Dr. David A. Freidel read and commented on my research in its dissertation form: their guidance (and patience) is much appreciated. Many thanks also to Dr. Christian Guksch and Dr. Michael Casimir for commenting on the ethnographic aspects of my work, and to the three anonymous reviewers for their many constructive comments. Thanks are also due to Frank Winchell for his generosity in providing information about the Butana Group ceramics.

Last but not least, I am greatly indebted to my wife Elisabet Bordt for taking care of the details of the manuscript preparation and for dealing with the editors during my prolonged absences. Many thanks are also due to the various editors at the University of Pennsylvania Press for their help, and for tolerating my frequent disappearance into the field.

Chapter I

On the Origins of Nomadism

> It is clear that without what they secure from the towns and traders of the farming country, the Beduin would have so one-sided a culture that they could not survive by it; no clothing, shelter, weapons, few utensils, limited diet. In one sense, accordingly, their own culture is no more than a half-culture. At least they can produce only half of it, and are dependent on the Hadhar, the "dwellers in brick," for the other half.
>
> Kroeber, *Anthropology* (278).

Kroeber's (1948) cultural view of nomads—focusing on their crucial linkage with sedentary peoples—has only a few followers among archaeologists and historians (cf., e.g., J. Klein 1921; Braudel 1973; Galvin 1987). Many more subscribe to the ecological perspective (Ibn Khaldun 1396 [1958]; Spooner 1972; Khazanov 1984), which emphasizes nomadism's adaptive advantage in arid lands over its economic function in herder/cultivator symbiosis. The ecologists claim that nomadism emerged and persists in uncultivable lands where a mobile, pastoral way of life was, and remains, the only viable subsistence strategy (Coon 1943; E. Bacon 1954; Lattimore 1967; R. McC. Adams 1974).

In this book I argue that the ecological view does not universally explain nomadism. On the basis of original research by the Butana Archaeological Project (BAP) and the Italian Archaeological Mission in Sudan, Kassala (IAMSK), and of a re-examination of the published archaeological sequences of Egypt, northern Sudan and northern Ethiopia from ca. 5000 BC onward, I will argue that nomadism in northeast Africa was, as Kroeber suggests, a part of a larger entity, a cog in the machinery of state administered, super-regional economic networks: in short, the ranching industry of the early states.

To set the stage for documenting these claims, the theoretical framework of the study is presented in this chapter along with the "symbiosis" model to explain the rise and persistence of nomadism in northeast Africa. To begin with, however, of the many possible points of entry into the discussion I have selected the most basic: proper definition of nomadism.

What is Nomadism?

Notwithstanding the frequent equating of nomads with just any mobile population (cf., e.g., Taylor 1972; Lee and deVore 1968; Oxenstierna 1967), most valid definitions speak of populations who are economically reliant on their herds and who wander seasonally in search of pastures (Spooner 1973; Goldschmidt 1979; Khazanov 1984). Other types of pastoralists are then variably defined as less reliant on herding, less mobile, or occupying richer environments where farming is feasible (cf., e.g., Cribb 1984; Murdock and Wilson 1972).

There are many ways to distinguish between actual nomads and other types of pastoral populations (for three examples see Appendix 1). Geographers, for instance, distinguish by the direction, length, and duration of seasonal herding cycles (Bernard and Lacroix 1906; Capot-Rey 1953; D.L. Johnson 1969). Others emphasize the ecology of the animals herded (Goldschmidt 1979), and yet others, patterns of pasture utilization or the particular segment of the population involved in herding (Barth 1962; Arbos 1923; also Khazanov 1984). Some distinguish pastoralist types by the permanence of their dwellings (E. Bacon 1954) or the presence or absence of riding animals (Goldschmidt 1979; Khazanov 1984). A few go to the other extreme by rejecting all attempts to distinguish nomads from pastoralists at large (N. Dyson-Hudson 1972; R. Dyson-Hudson 1972), or even wonder if the category "pastoral nomad" has any theoretical relevance at all (Asad 1979; Spooner 1973).

Assuming that nomadism exists and is theoretically relevant, for present purposes it must be defined in an archaeologically useful way to allow nomads to be clearly distinguished from other pastoralists in the northeast African prehistoric record. To this end a classification is proposed which, like Barth's (1973), takes as its point of departure the scale of specialized pastoral production in a given ethnic group.

Barth (1973; also Monod 1975) distinguished between: 1) an ethnic group composed of mixed economy households, with families both cultivating and herding domestic animals; 2) an ethnic group composed of two distinct segments, of which one specializes in agriculture and the other in pastoralism; and 3) two ethnic groups symbiotically forming one economic unit, wherein a nomadic one specializes in pastoral production and the other in agricultural production.

Following Barth's lead, true pastoral nomads can simply be defined as an ethnic group wherein everyone is directly or indirectly involved in pastoral production to the near exclusion of any other subsistence activity. Given the kinds of pastures available and the scale of pasture utilization, almost all such herding populations must engage in seasonal movement to feed their herds. The critical variable is not mobility but the demographic scale of specialized pastoral production.[1] "Ethnic group," however, is a slippery concept: archaeological cultures do not always represent an ethnically distinct population (Hodder 1982). For present purposes, the "ethnic" unity of the population is downplayed in favor of its more concrete demographic and geographic aspects: a regional population of several thousand souls inhabiting an area in the thousands of square kilometers.

A good ethnographic example of such a regional, nomadic population are the 11,300 strong Kababish tribe inhabiting 48,000 km^2 of the semi-arid Kordofan in western Sudan. They pursue pastoralism to the exclusion of any agriculture, trading for all the agricultural products they need with distant markets or with foreign traders in Kababish territory (Asad 1970).

Aside from the fully nomadic, three other types of pastoral population can be profitably distinguished. Of these, agropastoralists—Barth's two economic sectors in one ethnic group—have large segments of the population almost exclusively engaged in herding and others in agriculture. Some segments may even pursue a mixed subsistence strategy. In Africa, such large population segments are often lineages or clans, and sometimes castes. Considering, however, that clans, lineages, and castes are archaeologically difficult to distinguish, the segments are more usefully defined as geographically and economically distinct subgroups of a given regional population. Each subgroup comprises, according to ethnographic evidence, several hundred or a few thousand souls, inhabiting areas in the range of several hundred to a few thousand km^2.

A modern example of an agropastoral regional population are the 40,000 strong Beni Amer of Eritrea (a tribe of the Beja ethnic group), divided into 17 segments (clans), each 300–6000 strong (Nadel 1945). Every clan has a particular economy: some are camel herders, others herd cattle, sheep, and goats, and still others pursue horticulture. Many pursue a mixed economy, producing both agricultural and pastoral goods. The Beja Bisharin tribe of northeast Sudan, as another example, have their sedentary, agricultural Atbara tribal division, and camel and sheep herding Umm Ali and Umm Nagi divisions (Sandars 1933). Such agropastoral regional populations differ from the nomadic in that they cultivate crops and herd animals, and are thus at the regional scale self-sufficient in both pastoral and agricultural production. The nomads are not self-sufficient at this scale, but combined with an agricultural ethnic group can achieve self-sufficiency at a super-regional scale.

In another type of a regionally self-sufficient population—the mixed economy—every family is engaged in both herding and cultivation, and in African cases, often fishing as well (e.g., the Nuer, Jackson 1923; Evans-Pritchard 1940). In such mixed economy households pastoral and agricultural tasks are generally divided along sex lines, with the males herding and the females cultivating. Specialized production at such small scales means that, in contrast to agropastoralists, mixed economy populations are self-sufficient in both agricultural and pastoral production even at the household level.

Because identifying household level production can be archaeologically difficult, it may be more practical to assess production at the community (site) level, a compromise which will still allow mixed economy groups to be differentiated from agropastoral ones. A mixed economy population can then be defined by a regional set of sites, with each site containing evidence for both pastoral and agricultural production.

The last and also the least pastoral population is one wherein every member is almost exclusively engaged, directly or indirectly, in agricultural production. They are included in this classification only by virtue of the few domestic animals which almost every farmer keeps, much as almost every nomad dabbles in a little horticulture. The scale of such an agricultural population, like that of the nomadic, is a region with its several thousand inhabitants. A good example are the 20,000 Qemant of Ethiopia, inhabiting a territory of some 4000 km² just north of Lake Tana (Gamst 1969), all of whom, except priests and local officials, are directly or indirectly involved in agricultural production.

The idea of self-sufficiency highlights certain structural similarities among these four types of pastoral population. To illustrate, under the assumption that all populations need the primary and secondary products of both plants and animals (such as grain, bread, and beer, on the one hand, and meat, milk, and leather, on the other), the herding boy in a mixed economy household is as un-self-sufficient and dependent on the cultivator in the family as is the pastoral segment vis à vis the agricultural one in an agropastoral regional population. Symbiosis, however, between the herder and the cultivator—the meat and plant producing units—allows the creation of a self-sufficient economic unit at a larger scale which offsets the one-sidedness of the herder's adaptation. The scale of the self-sufficient economic unit is determined by the size of its specialized components. Thus specialized members in the household are capable of creating a family sized self-sufficient unit, while the segments of an agropastoral population can create self-sufficient units only at the multi-segment, or as in the case of the Bisharin, regional population scale.

The specialized pastoral nomadic regional population—Kroeber's no-madic half-culture—is similarly dependent for self-sufficiency on symbiotic links with a specialized agricultural regional population, to offset, at the proper scale, its economic one-sidedness. Because of the scale of its compo-nents, however, such a nomad/agricultural self-sufficient economic unit exists only at the super-regional, multi-cultural scale.

Evidence that northeast African nomads are linked to agriculturalists in just such symbiotic networks comes from many sources. Kroeber, speaking of Arabian Bedouin, articulates the point best. For the Rashaida and some of the Beja tribes of northeast Sudan, the camel-meat markets of Egypt are vital to their way of life. In Somalia, trade of livestock for the products of settled agriculturalists is an economic pattern which seems to have great antiquity (Swift 1979).

An exception, as far as the exchange of primary products (grain for meat) is concerned, may be the pastoral Masai of East Africa, who are reported to have relied exclusively on their herds with a diet predominantly of milk, which apparently even allowed them to place taboos on agricultural and other non-pastoral foods (Jacobs 1975). Such taboos, however, seem to have applied only to primary agricultural products. Jacobs (1975: 407 note 1) reports a lively trade in honey, medicine, and pottery with the Dorobo. Even so, the pastoral Masai may be an exception—indeed, the one which proves the rule. They are undoubtedly an atypical variety of African no-madic society (Jacobs 1975: 409).

Obviously the form and content of the symbiotic links connecting re-gional populations, segments, and family members differ significantly. In the last the link may be dependency, in the second reciprocity between kinsmen or, as in the first, commercialism. Other forms may include hired herders, client cultivators, and even occasional raiding—the last a form of relation which would be more antibiotic than symbiotic, and therefore probably employed only to offset temporary breakdown in symbiotic rela-tions (e.g., the Baluchi case reported in Salzman 1978). The farmer's few animals and the nomad's little garden may also be measures taken against the same eventuality. Another form, running caravans, may involve the exchange of pastoral services more than its primary and secondary products. Whatever the means and formal arrangements of symbiosis, the idea remains the same: that a specialized pastoral sector of the economy obtain the needed goods and services it does not itself produce.

Regardless of its varying forms and the differences in scale of specialized production and exchange, symbiosis structurally remains a means for allowing specialized producers to become part of a self-sufficient economic unit at the appropriate scale. This structural integrity with variations only along the dimension of scale suggests that perhaps the four types of pastoral adaptation are evolutionarily related, with the more complex, super-regional nomad/agricultural economic unit representing a highly refined, developed, and magnified version of the simple household level mixed herding/cultivating strategy.

The northeast African archaeological record, which shows mixed economies in the earliest neolithic period (see chapter 6), supports this idea of an evolution from less to more specialized pastoralism. Indeed, as shown below, all current theories on the subject assume such an evolution, although each postulates a different reason for the economic transformation.

Theories on the Origin of Nomadism

Apparently the earliest theory (perhaps even born of Sumerian speculation; see Kroeber 1948: 278) cast nomads as erstwhile hunter/gatherers who had domesticated their prey: a transformation of a technically mixed economy (but hunter/gatherer rather than herder/cultivator) population into a specialized nomadic one. Condorcet, Montesquieu, Morgan, and Engels were among many who subscribed to this view (Gellner 1984). Although it remained popular in the first half of this century (Schmidt and Koppers 1924; Flor 1930; Thurnwald 1932), the idea lost its appeal when Near Eastern archaeological finds showed that the transition from hunting/gathering first led to a broad based food-producing economy, wherein herding and cultivation as well as foraging and hunting played a part (Reed 1959; Braidwood 1960; Hole, Flannery, and Neely 1969).

A more resilient theory has been the ecological one which claims that erstwhile mixed economy populations who came to inhabit marginal lands were forced—because it was the only viable option—to forsake cultivation in favor of pastoral production, and thus became nomadic. As for how populations came to find themselves in marginal lands, some say deforestation or climatic change destroyed their arable lands (Barker 1981; Sherratt 1983; Geddes 1983), and others that force of arms or swelling numbers displaced them into existing arid zones (Coon 1943; Lattimore 1967; Service 1975). The popularity of these ecological ideas seems to rest partly on the fact that most modern nomadic populations inhabit such ecologically marginal lands.

In some ecological theories, however, factors other than the environment are considered instrumental. For example, the rapid exponential growth rate of herds—making animal stocks an economically more lucrative investment than crops—is thought by some to have led early neolithic mixed economy populations to full-time herding (Sauer 1952; Barth 1973; Gilbert 1983).

Such theories emphasizing nature's role have more recently been challenged by the cultural school, which considers nomadism a product of the social environment. A prominent faction within the cultural school claims that the nomad's mobility is a defense against more powerful, aggressive state governments (Ekvall 1961; Irons 1968; 1979; Shahrani 1979). Mixed economy hinterland populations under military threat from neighboring states are thus thought to have become nomadic principally to exploit the defensive advantage of mobility.

Another faction of the cultural school considers nomadism a pastoral industry which, along with many other specialized industries, emerged when state administered regional markets provided the incentive for populations to specialize in one or another economic pursuit (Braudel 1973; Lynch 1983; Galvin 1987). Yet another faction sees nomadic populations as the herders of an originally mixed economy group who were displaced when large scale irrigation technology prompted their expulsion out of the agricultural lands (Lees and Bates 1974).

These opposing cultural and ecological views have recently inspired researchers to attempt a theoretical synthesis, simultaneously implicating both factors as the causes of nomadism (Lynch 1983; Sherratt 1983; Rosen 1988; Khazanov 1984; Simmons et al. 1988). Generally, they claim that population pressure not only displaced groups into the hinterlands, but also led to the emergence of state societies and their regional markets, thus providing both motive and opportunity for the development of a specialized pastoral nomadic adaptation. Like the ecological theories, this one postulates the transformation of an originally mixed economy population into two independent groups, one pastoral and the other agricultural.[2]

In all the different views, the most commonly envisaged evolutionary trajectory is from a mixed economy population to a nomadic one. Some, like the proponents of the state market model, do not rule out the possibility that nomads arose out of an agropastoral population, but this intermediate type of adaptation is otherwise largely ignored. Understandably so, given that agropastoralists are not (with the notable exception of Barth 1973) explicitly acknowledged in most classifications.

By including agropastoralists, however, one can propose an evolutionary model of gradually increasing scales of specialized pastoral production and, consequently, of symbiosis between herding and farming components of a population. To reframe the question of the development of nomadism, then, one may ask what encouraged an intra-family symbiotic system to turn into a larger inter-segmental, and finally into an inter-regional symbiotic system, and above all, what sustained this quantum increase in scale of economic structure?

When the question is framed thus, the answers provided by the traditional theories can be seen to be too specific. Factors such as environmental change, herd growth and the profit motive, warfare, trade, and irrigation, may each be a specific historic stimulus which encouraged one or another population to give up everything for the cause of herding. None of the traditional theories, however, provides a general model to explain how the specialized production/symbiosis structure was thereafter maintained at the appropriate scale for centuries at a time. Such an explanation would require theory at a higher level of abstraction, one going beyond specific historic events.

The key to this higher level may be Kroeber's idea of the half-culture, as quoted at the beginning of this chapter. If it is accepted that without the means to obtain needed products from a settled agricultural society, nomadism—that is, fully specialized, large scale pastoral production—cannot exist in its pure form, it follows that neither the ecological nor some of the cultural factors invoked sustain this adaptation. At most, they deliver one of the many possible initial kicks toward nomadism. What, thereafter, allows the "kicked" population to remain nomadic, in view of the half-culture idea, must be the symbiotic links which satisfy its demand for the products of settled agricultural populations, and thus offsets its one-sidedness. Without this symbiotic link—as some scholars have already noted (Barth 1973; Bates and Lees 1977; Khazanov 1984)—the specialized nomads have no choice but to partially settle down to an agricultural life.

To the question what allowed a symbiotic structure the size of a family to ultimately turn into an exchange network spread over regions and including the several thousand families which make up the respective populations of a nomadic and an agricultural society, the obvious answer seems to be increased organization, administration, economic opportunities, and widening networks for exchange of products and information—in short, the development of politically, economically, and technologically more complex societies. The sheer scale of nomadic and agricultural societies linked in a long term symbiotic or exchange system would seem to require a level of economic co-ordination not commonly associated with societies less complex than an early state. Indeed, the early state's ability to co-ordinate forces at such scale remains a part of its definition (Wright and Johnson 1975; Service 1975; Cohen 1978).

A mixed economy society, on the other hand, could conceivably exist at any level of social complexity from the lowest tribal and band organization to a state level one. No matter how much administrative power and potential for information exchange, the mixed economy society utilizes only very low levels of either. It is the only level of symbiotic relationship possible in societies of low complexity, and if it occurs in a setting of higher complexity, it represents a less than optimal use of available organizational resources: essentially, a case of non-participation in regional economy.

Given these extremes, an agropastoral society should ideally exist at a medium level of social organization: one wherein production and exchange are coordinated at an intra-regional scale. Something like a chiefdom level of organization—less hierarchic and with a smaller demographic base and geographic extent than a state, yet more complex and administratively unified than a tribe—would seem to be a prerequisite for agropastoralism.

This is not simply to say that chiefdoms cause agropastoralism, or that states cause nomadism; rather, that agropastoralism is not possible with less than a chiefdom-like scale of organization, nor nomadism without the scale of administrative ability exhibited by early states.[3] In this sense, the general cause for the development of nomadism is attributed to the increased complexity of social, political, and economic systems. The immediate historic event which initially caused a specific population to become nomadic or agropastoral, on the other hand, can and undoubtedly did vary from time to time and place to place and probably included such factors as warfare, population displacement, and decreased agricultural potential of an area.

The proposed development of nomadism is neither unilineal nor unidirectional. The immediate causes can be many and varied, and the route to nomadism can also be different in each case. Furthermore, at least theoretically, once inter-regional symbiosis breaks down, nomads can "devolve" into the smaller symbiotic structure of an agropastoral or mixed economy population, again—one presumes—for a variety of possible immediate reasons and through one of several possible routes. Indeed, a population conceivably could evolve and devolve rapidly to and from nomadism.

Such short term tactical changes in adaptation, or failed attempts at maintaining a large scale symbiotic structure, are, however, ignored in the present study for two reasons. First, a society which was nomadic for, say, only a year or two could hardly be archaeologically visible: the data are too coarse-grained for that. Second, and more importantly, the present study is concerned with successful nomadic adaptations, those which existed for centuries at a time and which make the concept of nomadism theoretically relevant.

For similar reasons, the main concern here is the evolution from less to more specialized societies. Although there may have been isolated incidents to the contrary, what we know of the northeast African early neolithic, and today's adaptations shows that pastoralism has gradually become a more specialized industry. It is this trajectory which is here the focus of investigation.

The proposed explanatory model for this trajectory suggests an evolutionary staircase, with jumps from mixed economy to agropastoral and then to either agricultural or pastoral populations. These transformations may actually involve some minor stagelets along the way. Between the mixed economy stage and the agropastoral one, there may have been several intermediate forms of pastoralism with the scale of symbiosis gradually growing from an intra-family affair, to an inter-family one, to one between extended kin-groups, and then finally to a clan level characteristic of agropastoralism. Beyond that, there may have been as many forms through which a population transformed en route to true nomadism.

An example of such a stagelet between agropastoralism and true nomadism may be the Bisharin Beja of northeastern Sudan, who have three economically specialized tribal divisions, each including several clans (Sandars 1933). As such they represent a scale of symbiosis larger than the agropastoralists like the Beni Amer (Nadel 1945). Given the quality of data, however, such stagelets may not be archaeologically distinguishable from the main types discussed. Thus, for present purposes only the three main scales of symbiotic structure are considered. When appropriate, one can make adjustments to the model to include finer distinctions as well.

A northeast African nomadic regional population, it has been argued, is one half of a symbiotic structure, the other half of which consists of an "ethnically" separate, settled agricultural regional population. Nomadism evolved there in the context of increasing social, political, and economic complexity, albeit each nomadic transformation initially occurred for its own particular historical reasons, and through particular routes. To test these propositions archaeologically, it must be shown that there were developmental trajectories from mixed economy, through agropastoral, and finally to nomadic adaptations, and that these occurred in parallel with socio-political complexity evolving from relatively simple tribal-like organizations, to chiefdom-like intermediate levels of complexity, and finally to relatively complex early state organizations (Fig. 1.1). At the same time, it must be verified that specific factors such as environmental change, population pressure, exponential herd growth, conflict, and irrigation do not provide a general explanation for the emergence and continuation of nomadism in northeast Africa.

In the chapters ahead the archaeological evidence from the eastern Sudan is presented to show in detail the trajectory which led to the development of nomadism there. After that, the perspective is enlarged and the available archaeological evidence is presented showing other trajectories to nomadism from across northeast Africa. First, however, some of the methodological concerns for archaeologically identifying nomads are addressed in the following chapter.

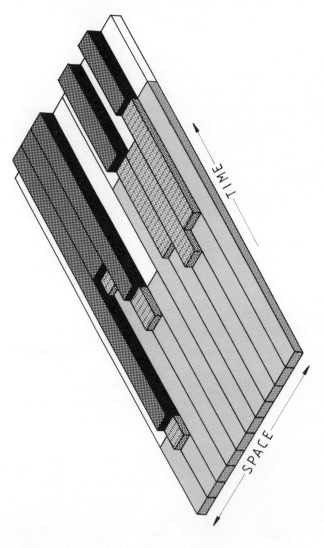

Figure 1.1. Illustration of the expected developmental sequence according to the symbiosis model, showing trajectories in ten neighbouring regions. *Darkest blocks*: agricultural regional populations; *dark gray, pinstriped blocks*: agropastoralists; *light gray blocks*: mixed economy poulations; *white blocks*: nomads. *One story high blocks* denote egalitarian societies; *two story blocks* denote ranked societies; *three story blocks* denote state level societies. Note the expected development of white blocks (nomads) on the boundaries of three story high black blocks (agricultural state level societies).

Chapter II

Identifying Nomads

Testing the theories for the origin of nomadism requires methods of distinguishing each of the four pastoral populations on the ground. Since the different kinds of adaptations, especially the nomadic and the agropastoral ones, can be properly documented only at the regional scale, the methodology must be based on large scale settlement pattern studies. Most of the traditional methods for identifying nomads are insufficient for present purposes as they generally address individual herder sites and not a regional adaptation. Nevertheless, as a first step toward interpreting the regional data such site-specific approaches are indispensable.

Traditionally, sites with a predominance of domestic animals in the faunal remains have been attributed to pastoralists. In some instances, researchers have tried to go further, to infer milk, meat, or wool production from the age and sex profile of the domestic animal remains (Chaplin 1969,1971; Hesse 1982,1984; Smith and Horowitz 1984). But faunal samples, so easily distorted by taphonomic processes, are rarely representative enough to allow such studies (Behrensmeyer and Hill 1980; Binford 1978, 1981; Giffford 1978, 1981; Klein and Cruz-Uribe 1984). Furthermore, most interpretations of animal mortality curves are based on a tentative model (Payne 1973) the validity of which has been challenged (Baker and Brothwell 1980; Collier and White 1976; Wilkinson 1976).

Faunal samples aside, the sites themselves can often reveal clues to the type of pastoralism practiced. Modern herders travel in small groups, carry little, and leave even less behind when they abandon camp (S.E. Smith 1980; Gifford et al. 1980; Robbins 1973). Thus, small sites with few artifacts and some domestic animal remains are often interpreted as camps of mobile herders (Connor 1984; Haaland 1981). Sometimes sites contain features such as tent outlines and stone alignments which match modern nomads' facilities (Hole 1974). Other useful features are animal enclosures (Chang and Koster 1986; Shimada and Shimada 1985).

Aside from its contents, a site's location can also be informative. Through catchment analyses of some East African sites, for example, Robertshaw and Collett (1983) identified those without immediate access to arable lands as herder sites (see also, Bower et al. 1977; Hole 1978, 1980; Zagarell 1983). Sometimes the location may indicate seasonal occupation (e.g., Haaland

1981; Sadr 1986). Features such as wind-breaks or even the placement of hearths can be similarly useful in places where wind direction varies from one season to another (Marks and Ferring 1971).

Burials have also proved useful. Analyses of human bone isotopes can allow the reconstruction of a herder's seasonal migratory pattern in addition to distinguishing him from a farmer (Sealy and Van der Merwe 1987; Caneva 1984; Coppa and Palmieri 1988).

Some of the above methods have been successfully applied to northeast African sites. One, however, can prove very misleading. As concerns the particular nature of a site, caution must be exercised in attributing all insubstantial sites with appropriate faunal remains to mobile herders. Most cultivators in the modern Sudan occupy homesteads, hamlets, and villages for a relatively short period ranging between five years (Uduk, James 1979) and the lifespan of the ranking members (ca. 50–100 years, Qemant for example, Gamst 1969). Without careful consideration, the remains of these sedentary but short term farming communities may be mistaken for those of a mobile herding population. The problem can only be compounded when cultivators keep domestic animals and even build enclosures for them (Qemant, Gamst 1969).

But even with careful consideration of the length of occupation at each site, most traditional methods do not suffice to distinguish between nomadic and agropastoral regional population. For that, regional site distributions must be examined. The ethnographic examples below serve to illustrate this.

Agricultural populations, for instance, can either inhabit nucleated, long-lived villages (a common enough pattern in the Near East) or live in more dispersed and short lived hamlets and homesteads, as is the custom with the Qemant of Ethiopia (Gamst 1969). In either case, an agricultural regional population should be identifiable by the distribution of all sites in more fertile areas, and by the absence of seasonal herder campsites. Although herders of a different population may seasonally occupy the territory of an agricultural population (e.g., the Kassala Beni Amer), it should be possible to stylistically recognize their material remains as foreign. Independent lines of evidence, such as the distribution of grinding stones, macro-botanical remains, and abundance and variety of pottery, can serve to support the settlement pattern data.

Like the agricultural, a mixed economy population such as the Uduk (James 1979), Berti (Holy 1974), Ingessana (Evans-Pritchard 1927), or Nyangatom (Tornay 1981), may inhabit nucleated villages or dispersed households for a long or a short time (Fig. 2.1). Like the agriculturalists, their main population centers are located in arable lands, but in addition they generally have an associated series of satellite herding camps dispersed at distances beyond 15–20 km from the main settlements: a distance which represents half a day's walk for the herds.

The young male herders in a mixed economy household, such as among the Nuer (Evans-Pritchard 1940), may move far and frequently, spending the entire dry season away from their families (Fig. 2.2). The families generally inhabit the main settlements year round, or in some cases move during the driest month into temporary fishing camps closer to the river (Jackson 1923; Evans-Pritchard 1940; James 1979; Logan 1918; Lewis 1972). Unlike the herding camps, these are restricted to the riversides, are occupied by both sexes and various age groups, and presumably contain materials and refuse associated with fishing, not herding.

In contrast to the settlement patterns of agricultural and mixed economy populations, those of the modern nomadic populations are quite distinct. All nomads' settlements are ephemerally or seasonally occupied. The Kababish during the wet season, for example, live in camps dispersed far and wide, but in the dry season the herders and their families gather around well-fields in an enormous conglomeration of clustered and isolated tents (Asad 1970). In such seasonally reoccupied locales, the camp membership changes annually, and as there generally are no fixed structures, the camp's internal layout varies from one year to the next, as well (Asad 1970; Owen 1937). As among the Baggara (Fig. 2.3), population mobility can be quite high. The camp which Cunnison (1966) studied moved 61 times in one year. Settlements of nomads can be very short lived.

A similar settlement pattern could be discernible, at a sub-regional scale, among the pastoral segments of an agropastoral regional population. A geographically distinct, more agriculturally oriented segment of the same agropastoral population, however, may exhibit a settlement pattern similar to that of the agricultural or even the mixed economy regional population. For instance, the agricultural Bisharin tribal division (a super-segment) occupies large, long term villages in riverside locations, while the pastoral divisions migrate in the hinterland (Sandars 1933). Likewise, some Beni Amer sections (Fig. 2.4) have a settlement system similar to ones described above for mixed economy populations. Others live as nomads. Agropastoral settlement patterns are thus distinguishable only at the regional scale, where sub-regional variations in settlement/subsistence strategies can be detected.

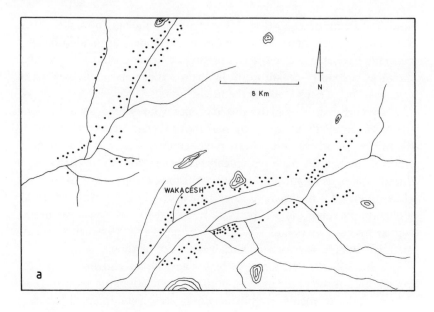

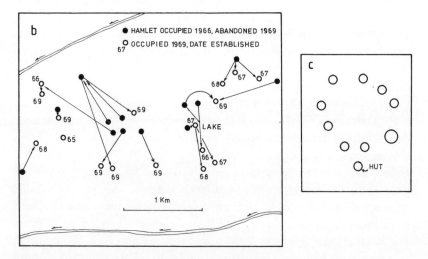

Figure 2.1. Uduk settlement patterns (after James 1979). a) northern Uduk settlements, 1968; b) hamlets of Wakacesh; c) Lake hamlet.

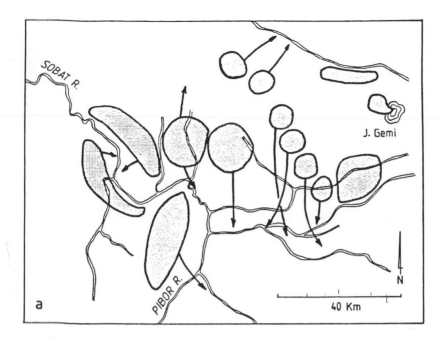

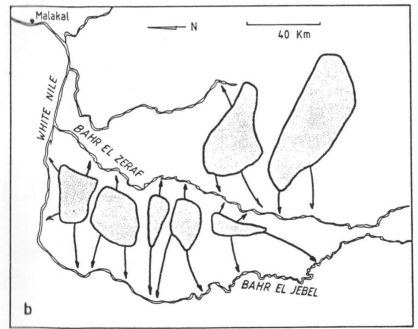

Figure 2.2. Nuer seasonal movements (after Evans-Pritchard 1940). a) dry season movements of the Eastern Jikany tribal sections; b) dry season movements of the Zeraf tribal sections.

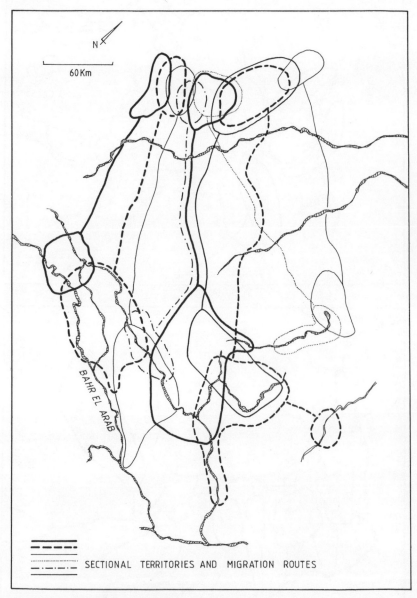

Figure 2.3. Humr Baggara tribal sections and seasonal movements (after Cunnison 1966).

down to 35–200 cm below surface. The high surface artifact densities, in conjunction with the subsurface deposits, indicate that deflation may have lowered the site surface until it was literally capped with a carpet of artifacts, which in turn prevented further deflation. The 200 cm of subsurface deposits at the site of Mahal Teglinos, as C14 dates indicate (Fattovich and Vitagliano 1989), represent about a millennium of occupation.

In contrast, the low density sites seem to represent seasonal camps. They have no in situ materials beneath their surface, and with the lowest densities of artifacts recorded in over 200 surveyed sites, they must represent the most impermanent category of occupation, which the ethnographic literature suggests are seasonal camps. In addition, general similarities were observed in the field between the surface aspects of these sites and of the recently abandoned seasonal camps of the modern herders, suggesting that the low density sites were indeed occupied for a very short time.

The majority of the sites in the survey fall between these high and low density extremes. For the sake of simplicity, they are described as medium density sites, although in reality they contain fairly high density concentrations of artifacts, separated by bare or low density areas. In all cases, about 5 cm of in situ materials could be found beneath the higher density parts of these sites. The alternating high and low artifact densities are interpreted as midden areas and cleared habitation zones. Compared with the high and low density sites, such sites appear to represent medium term occupations, corresponding to the ethnographically known settlements occupied anywhere from five years to a lifetime.

It might be thought that localities seasonally reoccupied by nomads would also leave behind a medium density site. The ethnographic data, however, suggest that this would not be the case. As among the Kababish (Asad 1970), nomads who return year after year to the same locality cover a very large area with scattered clusters of tents, none of which are built exactly on the same spot as last year's. This fact has important ramifications for distinguishing between such reoccupied localities and medium term occupations.

When a settlement is occupied consecutively for a number of years (medium term settlements), the fixed positions of the structures and facilities dictate that the areas where trash is deposited must also have fairly fixed positions. At the seasonally reoccupied localities, however, the very fact that the internal layout of the camp varies from year to year means that the trash disposal areas must likewise vary from one year to the next.

To illustrate, assume that both a medium term settlement of farmers and a seasonally reoccupied herder locality are inhabited for three years (Fig. 2.5). They may build up a more or less equal amount of archaeological deposits, but after deflation only the medium term settlement should still reveal the original middens. Since the midden locations never changed, there should be higher concentrations of artifacts in the middens and lower densities in the habitation and cleared areas. At the seasonally reoccupied locality, however, since the midden shifted every year, we might presume that the trash layout will have a random appearance, reflecting the compression of many different trash deposition loci. Such a deflated locality should show a relatively thin, even spread of artifacts over a large area: a sheet midden rather than cluster middens.

Thus, with few exceptions surface artifact densities at a site can differentiate between long, medium, and short term occupations. The exceptions may include cases like the Uduk (James 1979) whose extremely short lived hamlets (4–5 years) may come to resemble the remains of seasonal occupations. Perhaps the medium term settlements of a particularly untidy community could turn into a site with such random distribution of artifacts as to be indistinguishable from a seasonally reoccupied camp ground. The possibility of such misinterpretations, however, can be minimized if parallel, independent lines of evidence are used as well.

With combined settlement, faunal, and environmental data, regional populations can thus be identified as either mixed economy, agropastoral, agricultural, or nomadic. Such data were collected by BAP and IAMSK in the Southern Atbai region of the eastern Sudan. This region and its ancient climate and cultures are described in the next chapter along with the BAP/IAMSK field survey methods.

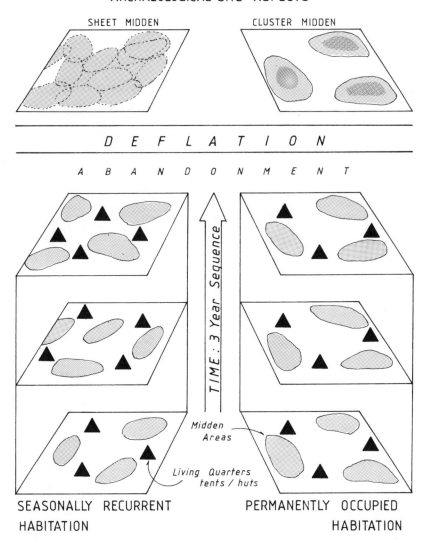

Figure 2.5. Sheet vs. cluster midden: hypothetical site-formation process.

Chapter III

The Natural and Cultural
Background of the Southern Atbai

Nestled between the Atbara River and the Ethiopian highlands, the Southern Atbai is today a borderland between desert in the north and cultivable lands in the south (Fig. 3.1). Here, 200–400 mm of rain per annum (Barbour 1964; Amin El-Tom 1975) support mainly acacias and scrub bushes. Broadleaf species are found only in the Gash river valley and its inland delta. Most of the Southern Atbai is today a vast clay plain only occasionally broken by lines of vegetation in a few shallow runoff channels. The only significant relief besides the jebels (rock outcrops) at the foot of the Ethiopian highlands is provided by the deeply incised valley of the Atbara, flanked by a stretch of eroded badlands known as the Karab (Fig. 3.2).

The Gash, Atbara, and Setit Rivers—the three main drainages of the Southern Atbai—flow in seasonal torrents from their catchments in the northern Ethiopian highlands, where rainfall is at least twice as high as in the Southern Atbai itself. Before the Atbara was dammed, it used to carry its load as far as the Nile during the rainy season. Now it is little more than a string of pools for most of the year. The Gash River, on the other hand, loses its waters in an inland delta stretching from around the town of Kassala over a hundred kilometers to the north. Except during the summer rainy season, the bed of the Gash is dry, but the water table remains consistently high throughout the year and can be easily tapped with shallow wells (Saeed 1969, 1972; Barbour 1964).

Geomorphological studies indicate that 5000–10,000 years ago, higher rainfall allowed the Gash to reach the Atbara (Coltorti et al. 1984; Durante et al. 1980; Cumming 1937; Barbour 1964). During the third millennium BC, however, drier conditions diverted its westward course to a natural basin north of Kassala, the present site of its silt choked delta (Barbour 1964).

At the very eastern edge of the Southern Atbai, scattered granitic outcrops mark the beginning of the Ethiopian highlands. The most prominent of these outcrops, the 700 meter high Jebel Kassala, is visible from at least

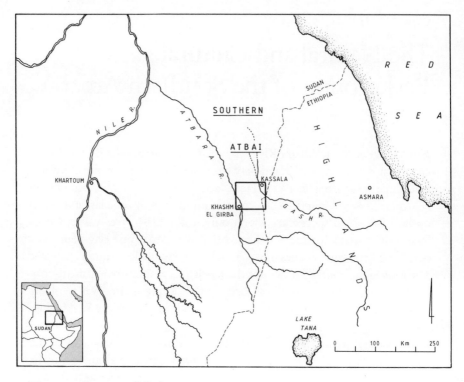

Figure 3.1. East central Sudan.

sixty kilometers away. Cumming (1937: 1), no doubt impressed by the sheer enormity of this bald, domed, pinkish mass of rock, described Jebel Kassala as a repulsive geologic phenomenon: a sentiment apparently not shared by the indigenous population, which has lived in the shadow of Jebel Kassala since at least the early third millennium BC. Today the town of Kassala, a provincial center, sits wedged between the Jebel and the Gash River.

Culturally, Kassala is a frontier zone. Located on the boundary of highland Ethiopia and lowland Sudan, it has been successively occupied since 1840 by Turko-Egyptians, Mahdists, and Anglo-Egyptian and Italian forces (Cumming 1937). Today the area around Kassala is inhabited by the Sudanese Ja'alin and by elements of several Beja tribes, including the Hadendowa, Beni Amer, and Halenga. Others, like the Arab Rashaida, recent immigrants from the Arabian peninsula, and Nigerian Muslims left behind on their way to (or if they were lucky, from) Mecca, as well as an assortment of refugees impart a tangibly frontier zone atmosphere.

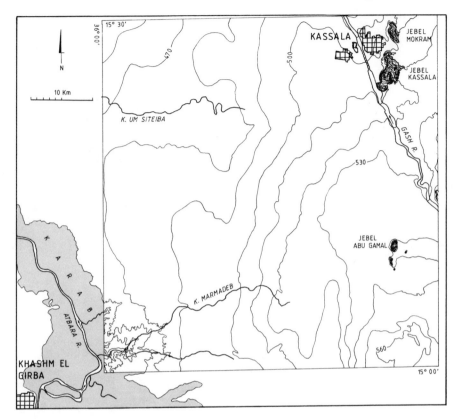

Figure 3.2. Geographical map of the Southern Atbai between Kassala and Khashm el Girba. Contour lines at 10 meter intervals.

Besides Kassala Town and a few smaller communities around it, the only other major population center in the region lies on the west bank of the Atbara at Khashm el Girba. The Atbara River forms a cultural boundary. Consequently, Beja and Rashaida are few in Khashm el Girba, whose population is mainly Shukriya and Lahawin Arab, as well as an assortment of Western Sudanese.

Between Khashm el Girba on the Atbara and Kassala on the Gash, the featureless steppe belies a great variety of local land use (Fig. 3.3). Generally speaking, the eastern side of the study area is better watered and more arable than the western side. The Gash River banks and its delta are the most fertile zones of the Southern Atbai. The delta in its natural state provides excellent grazing, and has long been the prize possession of the

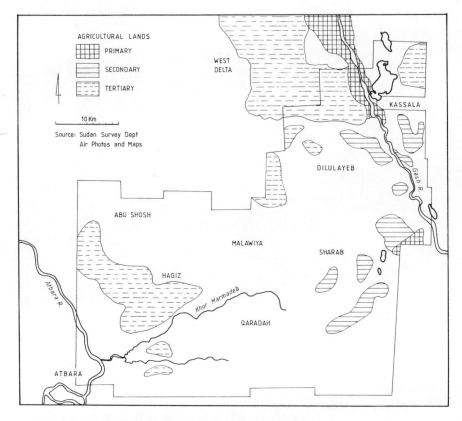

Figure 3.3. Agricultural lands of the Southern Atbai study area.

Hadendowa nomads (Barbour 1964). Most of its grazing potential is now lost to mechanized, irrigated cotton growing schemes, but the Hadendowa continue to profit as land owners. Just to the south, the banks of the Gash at the apex of the delta around Kassala Town are dotted with small garden plots growing a host of cash crops from sorghum to bananas (Barbour 1964).

The Sharab el Gash (literally, wine or drink of the Gash), some 35 kilometers south of Kassala Town, is the second most fertile zone of the Southern Atbai study area. It is inhabited by semi-sedentary and sedentary sections of the Beni Amer, who live in several large villages of thatch roofed huts. The Beni Amer cultivate small rainfed plots and pasture their herds within a short distance of the Sharab. Shallow well-fields, as at Habib Damar, provide water for most inhabitants.

Far to the west, the agricultural potential of the Atbara River banks may

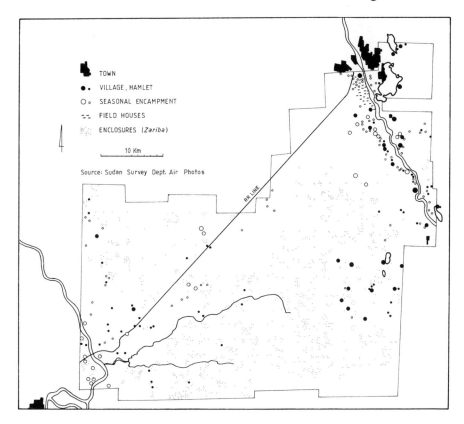

Figure 3.4. Modern settlements in the Southern Atbai study area.

be as high as that of the Sharab, but the floodplain is narrow and the fields are small and dispersed. Nowadays, the lowered river bed—a result of the Khashm el Girba dam—necessitates modern pump irrigation for farming: a luxury available only to few local inhabitants. The Shukriya Arabs, for example, cultivate small plots on the bar islands in the river. Nearer Khashm el Girba, on the west bank, small rainfed plots are cultivated by refugees and some locals living in thatch-roofed villages.

Away from the rivers, the Hagiz area and the paleo-delta (west delta) of the Gash River are crammed with small rainfed plots. These areas have the poorest agricultural lands and are cultivated by only a few local homesteads, and occasionally by nomads.

The intervening land between these arable zones—the steppe—is utilized by the herders from various tribes (Fig. 3.4). On air photos their herding camps, marked by thorn enclosures (*zaribas*) can be seen dotted all over the steppe and even into some of the less fertile agricultural areas. Several natural depressions in the steppe, as at Malawiya, Mitateb, and Abu Shosh, provide rain pools which seasonally attract nomads. At times, the area around these is choked with the black goat hair tents of the Rashaida. More dispersed are the Hadendowa mat tents, encountered in ones and twos all over the steppe.

The steppe has a few modern features as well. Isolated stations mark the road and rail link from Khashm el Girba to Kassala, and there are even a truck stop and a few shops at the Malawiya station. These, however, have done little to mar the traditional character of the land.

Paleo-environment

The Southern Atbai's landscape has changed only slightly over the last 3,000 years (Warren 1970; Wickens 1982). Before that, however, it was wetter (Fig. 3.5). Between 10,000 and 5,500 BC, during the early Holocene wet phase, north Africa enjoyed a pluvial climate. Lakes dotted what is now driest Sahara (Petit-Maire 1979). Since then there have been several oscillations from wet to dry and back. Thus, the early Holocene wet phase was succeeded by the mid-Holocene arid phase, which was followed by the Neolithic humid phase, the post-Neolithic arid phase, the post-Neolithic humid phase, and finally the present arid phase (Muzzolini 1982).

Wickens's (1982) paleo-environmental reconstruction (Fig. 3.6), based on botanical evidence, shows that during the early Holocene wet phase (ca. 10,000–5000 BC) the Southern Atbai was a deciduous savanna woodland: essentially an extension of the flood region which is now confined to the southern Sudan. In the middle Holocene (3000–1000 BC) it became a savanna. Thereafter the continued drying trend brought semi-desert to the northern half of the Southern Atbai.

This sequence of change, however, provides only a general backdrop. The details must be understood in terms of the Southern Atbai local hydrology. That the Gash River originally flowed as far as the Atbara has been known for some time (Cumming 1937; Barbour 1964). Recent geo-morphological investigations have confirmed this, showing that during the early Holocene wet phase the Gash formed a tributary of the Atbara, and was therefore part of the overall Nile drainage system (Durante et al. 1980; Coltorti et al. 1984). The ancient confluence of the Gash to the Atbara

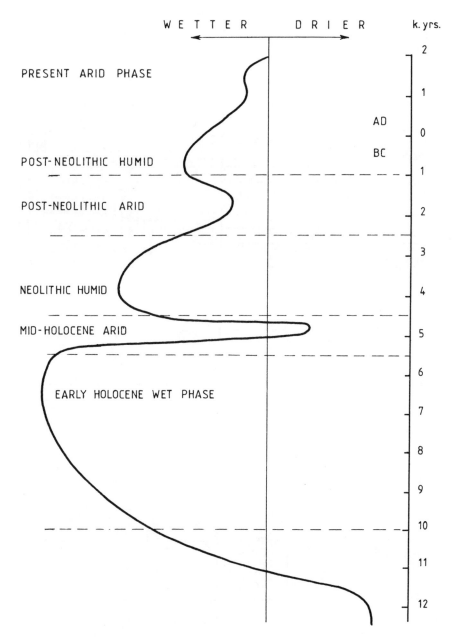

Figure 3.5. Chart of north African paleo-climates (after Muzzolini 1982).

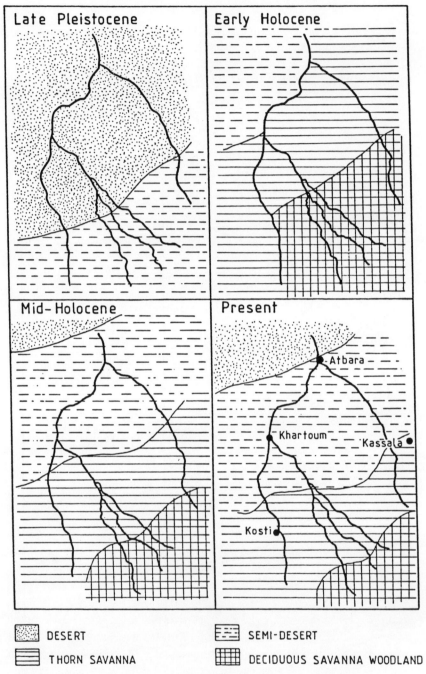

Figure 3.6. Paleo-environmental reconstruction of the central Sudan (after Wickens 1982).

Rivers can best be seen on Landsat imagery (Fig. 3.7a). This evidence and the geomorphological investigations suggest that the gradual climatic drying trend and the consequent reduction in the water flow caused the silting of the Gash River's older channels. This in turn caused the river to swing first to the northwest, and finally north to its present bed, which flows from the Ethiopian border to the inland delta north of the town of Kassala (Marks and Sadr 1988).

Figure 3.7b shows a reconstruction of the Gash paleo-channels, and their approximate age as deduced from site locations. Although it is not known how many of the channels were simultaneously active, the dates indicate that for a long time during the early Holocene period the Gash flowed west from around Jebel Abu Gamal to the Atbara via what is now the Khor Marmadeb. Between ca. 3000 and 2000 BC—i.e., with the transition from the Neolithic humid phase to the post-Neolithic arid phase—the Gash River changed course. Judging by the stratigraphic position of the first appearance of riverine and aquatic fauna in a major site at the base of Jebel Kassala (Coltorti et al. 1984), the river assumed its present course by ca. 2000 BC. The transition in the Gash hydrography was thus relatively rapid, and dramatically changed the local environment of the Southern Atbai study area. The erosion of the Atbara River valley probably began during the post-Neolithic arid phase, as well. No sites older than the first millennium BC (except for some Acheulean occurrences) have yet been found in the *karab* proper: they must have been destroyed by erosion.

The Southern Atbai Survey

This erosion has not compromised the survey. Indeed, it has facilitated matters by exposing sites of all periods since the early Holocene. Site destruction seems to be limited to the Karab, the Gash Delta, and the heavily populated areas of Kassala Town and Khashm el Girba. Even in the traditionally farmed areas, sites seem to have survived more or less intact.

The BAP survey around Khashm el Girba and the IAMSK survey in the Kassala area were carried out over the course of four seasons in 1981, 1982, and 1984 (Fig. 3.8). Since it was expected that the ancient inhabitants of the area were fairly mobile, reconstruction of the settlement systems required that surveys be as extensive as possible, covering all ecological zones from the river valleys to the hinterlands. To this end the study area was divided

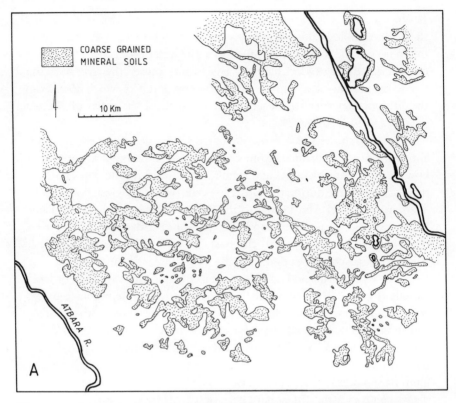

Figure 3.7. Ancient hydrography of the Southern Atbai. A) Distribution of coarse-grained mineral soils, as seen on NASA Landsat imagery.

into eight sectors (see Fig. 3.3). Attempts were made to survey each sector as fully as possible (Table 3.1).

During the first season, it seemed that sufficient time and funds would be available to survey the study area completely. Subsequently, however, political and logistical problems shortened the field seasons. A reevaluation of strategy became necessary. In order to meet the principal aim—extensive coverage—sample areas of each sector were rapidly surveyed in the hope that the gaps could be filled as additional time, funds, and fuel became available. In areas where the probability of site destruction was high, surveys were kept to a minimum. Eventually, circumstances led to the termination of surveys in 1984, and coverage was arrested at the stage shown in Figure 3.8.

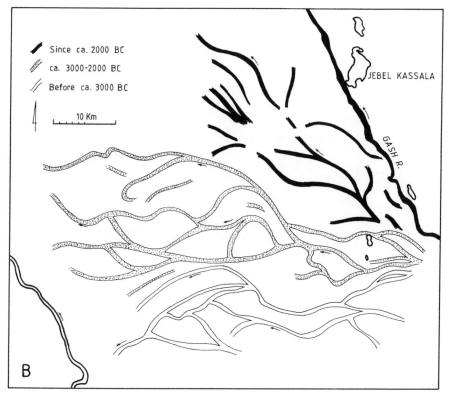

B) Reconstructed paleo-channels of the Gash River.

The configuration of survey transects was determined by each sector's terrain. In Dilulayeb, for example, flat, open ground allowed a semblance of systematic transect surveys. Of seven days allotted to this sector, each day was spent in a particular portion driving north/south or east/west transects by dead reckoning (i.e., with the aid of a mounted compass and the odometer: in such a featureless landscape aerial photographs were all but useless). Detailed logs were kept of the routes traveled, and the location of sites was additionally recorded by triangulation off surrounding jebels.

Since dead reckoning is a relatively imprecise navigational method, the transects never conformed to a truly N/S or E/W pattern. Only at the end of the day, when the sites were plotted onto maps, could the exact configuration be reconstructed. After the daily plotting, additional locales in need

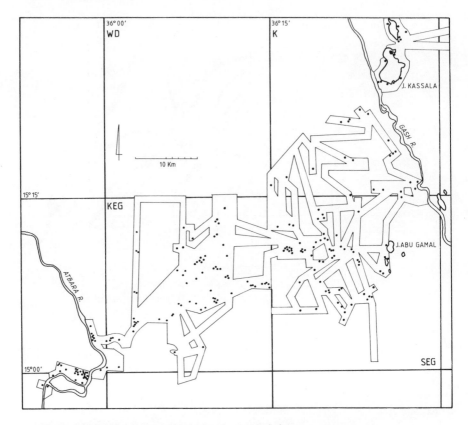

Figure 3.8. Southern Atbai survey and recorded sites.

of survey could be singled out and attended to on the following day. In this way the sector was surveyed with more or less even, though loose coverage. Indeed, plans were being made to tighten coverage in the Dilulayeb when a shortage of petrol forced the termination of surveys there.

The surveys in the Malawiya, Hagiz, and Abu Shosh sectors proceeded along much the same lines, except that less time was spent on the latter, and more on the former two sectors. In the Sharab, on the other hand, the scrub-choked paleo-channels of the Gash River as well as the many agricultural fields prevented the use of dead reckoning as a sampling device. Instead, transects had to be driven along existing tracks, and surveys were carried out in clearings encountered along these. Here, aerial photographs were more useful for planning and navigation. Similar procedures were followed in the Qaradah sector.

Table 3.1. The Southern Atbai Survey

Sector	Area (km²)	Coverage (km²)	Coverage (%)
Atbara	135	45	33.3
Abu Shosh	115	35	30.4
Hagiz	115	97	84.3
Qaradah	136	45	33.0
Malawiya	212	115	54.2
Sharab	280	135	48.2
Dilulayeb	349	166	47.2
Kassala	140	20	14.2
Total	1482	658	44.4

In the Atbara River valley vehicles could not be used effectively. Nor did the density of sites warrant their use. The allotted time for survey was spent recording sites within walking distance of each other. Little of the karab was surveyed. Likewise, in the Kassala sector urbanization, high population densities, and the profusion of agricultural fields and gardens restricted the survey to the bases of Jebels Kassala and Mokram.

Overall, the surveys were carried out as systematically as logistics permitted. In the end, the survey did achieve its primary goal of at least loosely covering all sectors of the study area. The extensive and rapid coverage was made possible by the extremely high site visibility afforded by the gravel-free clay plains of the study area. The largest sites were plainly visible from as far away as two kilometers. Smaller sites were visible from at least 500–1000 m away, while even the smallest sites could be easily seen from 200–300 m. Thus, as an average, the width of the transects surveyed has been computed at 1 km, reflecting a 500 m visibility range on each side of the route driven. In all, of the roughly 1500 km² which make up the study area, transects covered over 600 km².

The transect surveys led to the recording of 223 sites, many of which have more than one component. Because of the paucity of diagnostic artifacts, 33 of these sites could not be assigned to a particular part of the cultural sequence. All the rest could be placed, generally on the basis of decorated ceramics, although plainwares with diagnostic paste, slip, and/or rim forms, characteristic lithics, and polished stones were occasionally relied on as well.

In total, fifteen sites were excavated or tested by both projects. Of the remaining sites, over 80 percent were surface collected. The collections were generally carried out by a team of two workmen walking over the entire site for about half an hour. Initial attempts at collecting systematically within set grids turned up far too many unrecognizable small eroded sherds, and too few diagnostic ones: the unsystematic general surface collections proved far more effective.

The excavated and collected materials, along with a series of radiocarbon dates, permitted a reconstruction of a long cultural sequence (Fig. 3.9). Its details have been described elsewhere (Fattovich, Marks, and Mohammed-Ali 1984; Marks, Mohammed-Ali, and Fattovich 1986; Marks and Sadr 1988). Here, only a brief summary is presented of the part dealt with in this study (ca. 4000 BC–AD 500). In the common terminology adopted by the two projects, this period covers the early, middle, and late Kassala Phase, as well as the Taka Phase.

The Early Kassala Phase

All the sites of the early Kassala Phase belong to the Butana archaeological group. This group is defined by a specific ceramic assemblage which includes scraped pots, fine red-mouthed wares with incised herringbone pattern decoration on the body, and a few other characteristic types (Frank Winchell, personal communication). Exotic artifacts such as lip plugs and mace-heads made on imported porphyry are fairly abundant (Marks, Mohammed-Ali, and Fattovich 1986). The characteristic lithics include stone picks (examples of which are illustrated in Shiner 1971a, Part II, figures 10 a–c and figure 12 f), polished axes, perforators on flakes, and denticulated end-scrapers. Bi-polar flaking technique was common (Anthony Marks and Steven M'Butu, personal communication).

The Butana Group sites which date between ca. 4000 and 3000 BC apparently were occupied during the North African Neolithic Humid Phase (Table App. 2.1). Rainfall in the Southern Atbai at that time would have been ca. 400–600 mm per annum (Warren 1970). The Butana Group sites, principally located along the Atbara River and the Khor Marmadeb (Fig. 3.10), were presumably occupied at a time when the Gash River flowed west across the steppe as far as the Atbara.

Only nine Butana Group sites have been recorded in the survey (Table App. 2.2). Five of these were found by Shiner during his reconnaissance of

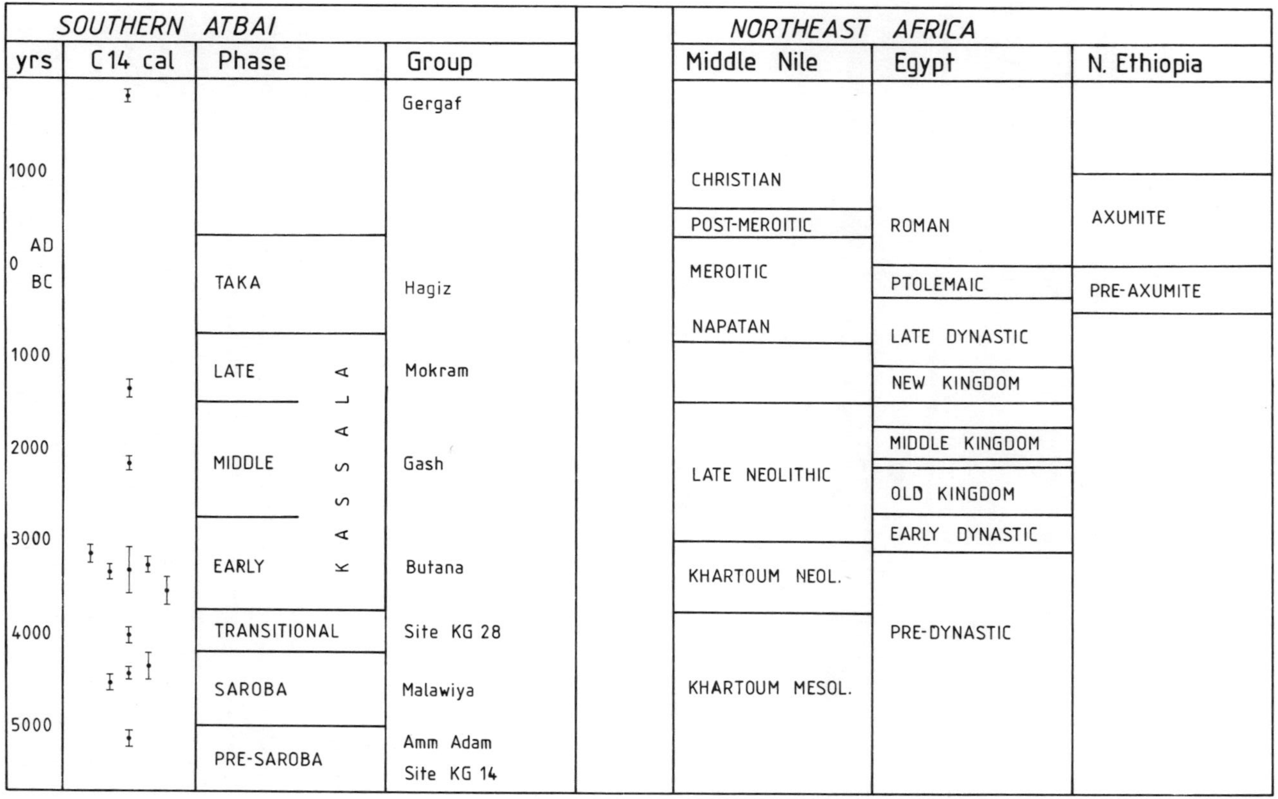

SOUTHERN ATBAI

yrs	C14 cal	Phase	Group
1000 AD			Gergaf
0 AD/BC		TAKA	Hagiz
1000 BC		LATE	Mokram
2000		MIDDLE	Gash
3000		EARLY	Butana
4000		TRANSITIONAL	Site KG 28
		SAROBA	Malawiya
5000		PRE-SAROBA	Amm Adam / Site KG 14

KASSALA spans LATE, MIDDLE, EARLY phases.

NORTHEAST AFRICA

Middle Nile	Egypt	N. Ethiopia
CHRISTIAN	ROMAN	AXUMITE
POST-MEROITIC	PTOLEMAIC	PRE-AXUMITE
MEROITIC	LATE DYNASTIC	
NAPATAN	NEW KINGDOM	
	MIDDLE KINGDOM	
LATE NEOLITHIC	OLD KINGDOM	
	EARLY DYNASTIC	
KHARTOUM NEOL.	PRE-DYNASTIC	
KHARTOUM MESOL.		

Figure 3.9. Cultural sequence of the Southern Atbai and select regions of northeast Africa.

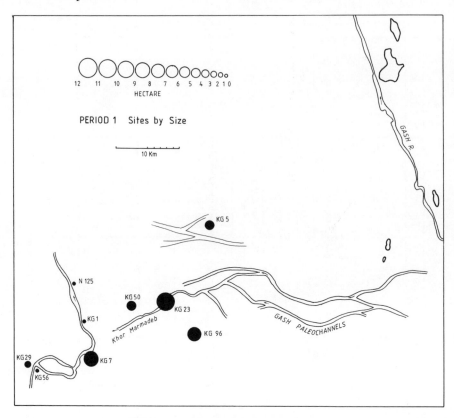

Figure 3.10. Butana Group site distribution.

the Khashm el Girba area during the late sixties (Shiner 1971 a). The BAP has tested six of the Butana Group sites. The excavations have shown that the five largest, ranging in size from two and a half to over 10 hectares, had deposits from a half to over two meters deep. Several chunks of daub found in the two deepest sites indicate that durable structures were constructed, fortifying the impression of a nucleated and sedentary resident population.

The excavated Butana Group faunal remains indicate that hunting was a major focus of subsistence (Table App. 2.3). Sites along the Atbara River contain aquatic fauna as well. Bones of domesticated cattle and small livestock have been found but only in the strata and sites which date to the later half of this phase (Peters 1986). Numerous grinding stones and the stone picks which may have been used for ground breaking suggest cultivation (Shiner 1971a: 341; and Steven M'Butu personal communication). Seeds embedded in Butana Group ceramic sherds have been identified as sorghum and millet, but it is not yet known whether they were domesticated (D'Andrea and Tsubakisaka 1990)

The Middle Kassala Phase

The middle Kassala Phase is known to a large extent from excavations carried out at the site of Mahal Teglinos by the Italian Archaeological Mission. A suite of dates from this site show that the phase lasted from ca. 3000 to 1500 BC (Table App. 3.1). The archaeological group of this phase is known as the Gash and differs from the Butana in several respects. Although the Gash Group ceramic assemblage is dominated by scraped sherds (D'Alessandro 1985), these differ in paste, temper, and firing from the Butana Group scraped ceramics. Other vessels of the Gash Group are generally decorated by punctations, roulettes, or incisions in a narrow band around the rim (Fig. 3.11, a–f). In the uppermost layers of Mahal Teglinos a wide rim band of incised motif is also present (Fig. 3.11,g,h). The ceramics from the lower strata of Mahal Teglinos belong to smaller vessels which were generally left undecorated. These differences between the upper and lower half of the deposits at Mahal Teglinos allow other sites of the Gash Group found during the survey to be dated relatively. As it happens, almost all of these seem to date to the latter half of this phase.

Aside from the ceramics, there are many ground and polished stone tools, but none of the characteristic Butana Group picks nor the maceheads. The Gash Group lithics currently remain under analysis.

So far, 31 Gash Group sites have been recorded in the survey (Table App. 3.2). Their location (Fig. 3.12) in the eastern half of the steppe and along the modern Gash River is best explained by the progressive change in the paleo-Gash River's course. The sites range in size from less than a hectare to over 12 ha. The largest Gash Group sites have over 2 meters of in situ deposits, indicating stable, long term occupation (Fig. 3.13). Other Gash Group sites are surficial, or have only 5–10 cm of depth.

Excavations at Mahal Teglinos (K 1) revealed a faunal assemblage including reptiles, foxes, jackals, hares, porcupines, and rodents. Wild bovids such as gazelle and dikdik were also present. Aside from these hunted animals,

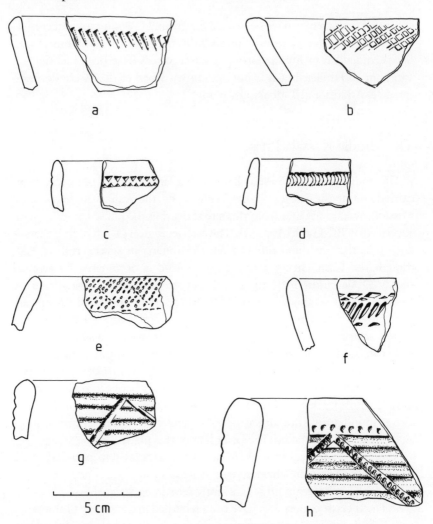

Figure 3.11. Some rim band decorated sherds of the Gash Group.

the greater part of the bovid materials represented domesticated forms including cattle, goats, and sheep (Geraads 1983). Riverine and river edge animals such as molluscs, catfish, hippopotami, and warthogs were found only in the upper half of the deposits at Mahal Teglinos, perhaps indicating the time when the river finally reached its present bed, thus entering the site's catchment.

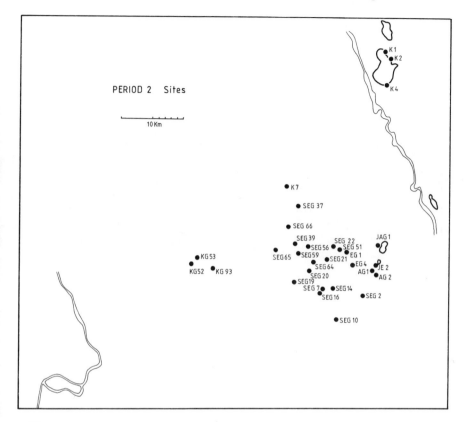

Figure 3.12. Gash Group site distribution.

Numerous grinding stones, grinding holes in bedrock, clay lined storage pits, and actual remains of *Hordeum* sp., *Ziziphus* sp., and *leguminosae* (Costantini et al. 1983) indicate that cultivation played a role in the Gash Group's subsistence as well.

Mahal Teglinos contains many informative features. In one area a sequence of 15 floors were marked by baked soils and hearths. In the two uppermost floors, possible structures were identified. Traces of postholes were recorded in the lower strata (Fattovich 1984c). The surface of Mahal Teglinos's eastern half, and that of the northern half of another large Gash Group site, JAG 1, are covered with dozens of small stone tumuli each about a meter in diameter. One excavated at Mahal Teglinos proved to be a circle built of two or three courses of rock and enclosing a heap of grinding

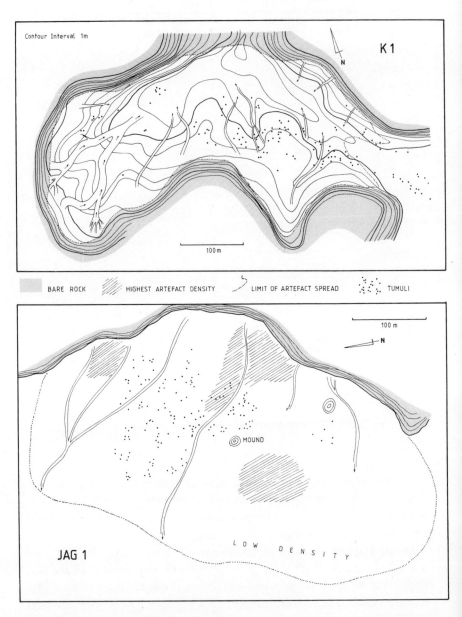

Figure 3.13. Gash Group sites K1 and JAG1.

implements. The function of the stone circles remains enigmatic, but a funerary association seems unlikely (Fattovich 1984c). Other excavations have revealed a cemetery in a part of Mahal Teglinos, where burials were marked with larger stone circles of various diameters and plain monolithic stelae each about a meter tall. By the end of the 1986 season 35 stelae were found associated with 24 burials within a 92 m² excavation area (Fattovich 1989). Although none of the graves contained any burial goods, the use of stelae (exclusively at Mahal Teglinos) may indicate some form of social ranking. Similar stelae were seen as far afield as Aqiq on the Red Sea coast near the Ethiopian border (Fattovich 1989), which may indicate something of the geographical spread of this group.

Another indication of its spread comes from the site of Agordat in northern Ethiopia, about 150 km east of Kassala, where Arkell (1954) uncovered ceramics which now can be identified stylistically as those of a Gash Group population.

This cultural spread from Kassala to the Red Sea coast, and the resources available in this area have led Fattovich (1985) to the tentative conclusion that Mahal Teglinos was the overland port of trade of the land of Punt, a famous trading partner of ancient Egypt. Among the many clues, probably the most significant are the sherds and few seals found at Mahal Teglinos which are identical to examples found at Kerma (Fattovich, Sadr, and Vitagliano 1988), thought to have been the intermediary agent in the Egypt-Punt trade network before 1500 BC.

The Late Kassala Phase

The late Kassala Phase, despite its different archaeological (ceramic style) Group—the Mokram—essentially represents a continuation of the middle Kassala Phase occupation. The Mokram Group is characterized by black-mouthed red slipped ceramic wares often decorated with cross-incised net-patterns (Fig. 3.14, a,b) or parallel groove-carved lines (Fig. 3.14, c,d). Fine red-slipped and burnished wares are sometimes decorated with various rim-band motifs (Fig. 3.14, e,f). There are, in addition, a host of minor types (Fig. 3.14, g,h), among which are some similar to the ceramics of the Gash Group (Sadr 1990). The Mokram Group lithics, mostly made on agate, include few formal tools (Banks, ms.). Grinding implements and certain characteristic polished porphyry bracelets are found on almost all sites of this phase.

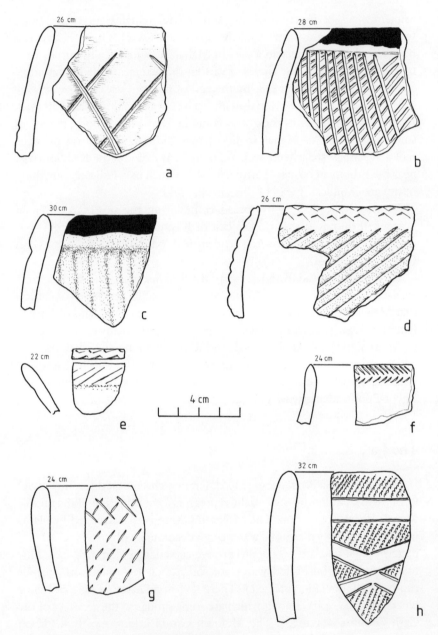

Figure 3.14. Some characteristic Mokram Group ceramic decorations.

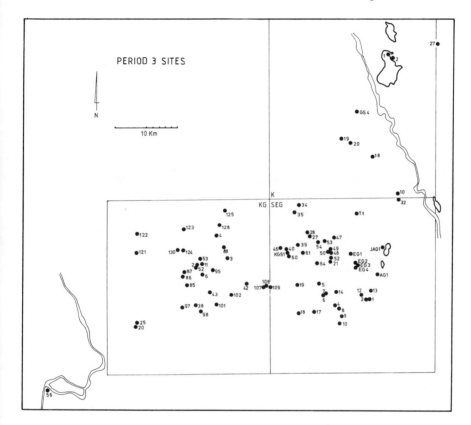

Figure 3.15. Sites of the Mokram Group.

Besides the continued production of some Gash Group ceramics, the continued occupation at 15 of the 31 middle Kassala Phase sites suggests that the inhabitants of the Southern Atbai stayed in place through the transition to the late Kassala Phase (Fig. 3.15). Among these sites were the two major ones of the Gash Group, Mahal Teglinos and JAG 1, both of which remained occupied after 1500 BC (Table App. 4.1).

This continued occupation along with the change in material culture has been interpreted as a cultural takeover by a population from the Northern Atbai known archaeologically as the Pan-Grave culture (also known in Egyptian texts as the Medjay, Bietak 1966), whose ceramic assemblage is practically identical to the Mokram's (Sadr 1987, 1990). The population of the Southern Atbai, around 1500 BC, seems to have become Medjay without any noticeable influx of actual Medjay from the North (see also chapter 7).

Ceramic seriations (Figure App. 4.1) show that the late Kassala Phase can be divided into an early and a late component. The ceramics of the late Mokram Group resemble the typical ones but have more fiber tempering and less decorational variety, in addition to some changes in the placement of designs (Sadr, ms.).

Floral remains and the imprints of seeds in burnt clay from sites JAG 1 and SEG 9 indicate that sorghum was cultivated (Costantini et al. 1983). Faunal remains from three typical Mokram Group sites show that some animals such as gazelle and giraffe were hunted, but most remains belong to domesticated cattle, goat, and sheep. Fish remains are rare (Peters 1986) (Table App. 4.2).

The beginning of the late Kassala Phase can be securely dated to around 1500 BC from Mahal Teglinos, where C14 dates indicate that Gash Group occupation ended and Mokram Group began about that time. A C14 date, 3050 ± 90 BP, MASCA calibrated to 1350 BC, recovered from a different Mokram Group site, is in agreement (KG 20—then N 120—dated by Shiner 1971a).

The terminal date of the Kassala Phase, however, is not well documented. Sedimentation rates at Mahal Teglinos (not the most precise method of dating) suggest that the Mokram Group occupation there may have ended between 1100 and 1000 BC. Given that a late Mokram occupation followed in the Sharab area (but not around Kassala), the terminal date of the phase can probably be pushed into the early first millennium BC.

The Taka Phase

The settlements of the Taka Phase Hagiz Group (Table App. 5.1) are scattered throughout the study area (Fig. 3.16), often as intrusive components on earlier sites, and are easily recognized by characteristic pink/orange fiber tempered pottery. Most of these were undecorated, but those with decoration sported rim-band designs and scraped surfaces reminiscent of the middle Kassala Phase Gash Group ceramic designs. Relative to the earlier assemblages, however, the ceramics of the Hagiz Group were poorly made and carelessly decorated.

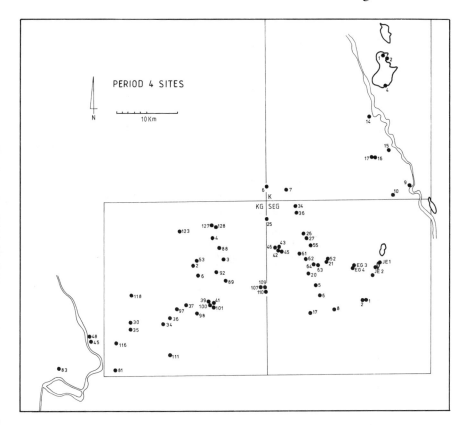

Figure 3.16. Sites of the Hagiz Group.

The Hagiz Group lithics do not greatly differ from those of the Mokram (Banks, ms.), but grinding stones are practically absent (see chapter 4). Polished stone artifacts are likewise infrequently found.

Faunal remains are also rare. The few bones recovered belong predominantly to domesticated forms (Joris Peters, personal communication). Macro-botanical remains were not encountered.

The Taka Phase is dated only on the strength of indirect evidence. Some pre-Axumite sherds found on Hagiz Group sites suggest an early to mid-first millennium BC date (Fattovich, Marks, and Mohammed-Ali 1984). A terminal date for the phase may be indicated by an Axumite text of King Ezana II, who apparently, after a battle won at Kemalke ford (probably just north of present day Khashm el Girba : Kobischchanov 1979), rounded up the local population (elements of some six tribes, comprising four thousand souls: Kirwan 1974) and deported them to the southern borders of the Axumite kingdom (Kobischchanov 1979). Perhaps the hiatus in the occupation of the Southern Atbai after the Taka Phase can be attributed to Ezana's raid. The phase ended, in any event, before the mid-first millennium AD: the few early Christian remains found at the base of Jebel Kassala bear no resemblance to those of the Hagiz Group (Rodolfo Fattovich, personal communication).

In the next chapter pertinent data are discussed to document the rise of nomadism in the Southern Atbai during the Taka Phase. It will be shown that the actual sequence of events there is a very close match to the hypothetical sequence generated by the symbiotic model.

Chapter IV

Nomads in the Southern Atbai

Test Implications of the Symbiosis Model

To confirm the symbiosis model, the developmental sequence in the Southern Atbai should be as follows. In the earliest phase—which would date to immediately after the introduction of domesticated animals into the regional economy (in the Southern Atbai, during the second half of the early Kassala Phase, see previous chapter)—populations should pursue a mixed subsistence strategy. Their settlements, whether nucleated or dispersed, should be located in the most favorable parts of the study area, which in the Southern Atbai would have been the Atbara and paleo-Gash river valleys. All settlements should show that both pastoralism and cultivation were practiced by the members of each community.

To be in keeping with the model, evidence should indicate that sociopolitical organization of the population in the earliest phase was fairly simple, with no evidence for great inequalities in rank and wealth. In archaeological terms, there should be negative evidence for administrative hierarchies among sites (G. Johnson 1981), negative evidence for unequal distribution of exotic artifacts among sites, and negative evidence for unusually rich burials. As will be shown in the following pages, the Butana Group of the early Kassala Phase, and possibly the Gash Group of the first half of the middle Kassala Phase sites, fit all the above requirements.

In the middle stages of the hypothetical sequence of the symbiotic model, with the beginning of more complex social, political, and economic organization, it is expected that the regional population becomes more diversified, and more specialized in pastoral and agricultural production. In archaeological terms, the data should indicate some inequality in distribution of exotics (wealth), rich burials, and evidence for specialized administrative activities (seals and stamps, perhaps). Settlement patterns should show some hierarchic ranking among sites.

To document the existence of the specialized pastoral and agricultural segments, sites must be found in both the river valleys and the steppe. The regional distribution of relevant faunal and macro-botanical remains, and the distribution of features such as corrals, stylistic elements of pottery, and even specific differences in settlement types and distributions should delineate boundaries between groups of sites in areas corresponding in scale to that of ethnographically known segments of an agropastoral population. As will be shown below, the Mokram Group of the late Kassala Phase and possibly the Gash Group population from the second half of the middle Kassala Phase fit the above requirements.

In the final phase of the hypothetical trajectory proposed by the symbiotic model, the regional population of the Southern Atbai is supposed to become specialized nomadic pastoralists as state level societies arise in neighboring regions. In archaeological terms, the regional settlement pattern in this final phase should show short term camp settlements everywhere, evidence for pastoral production, and negative evidence for substantial agriculture. It must be shown that the camps in the study area are not remains of a herding segment of an otherwise agropastoral regional population.

Nomadism should not appear earlier than the neighboring state. In the eastern Sudan this would be no earlier than 750 BC, when the Kushitic Kingdom was established in the Middle Nile Valley (Bradley 1984), or before the pre-Axumite kingdoms appeared in northern Ethiopia during the mid-first millennium BC (Fattovich 1984d) (see also chapter 8). Material evidence indicating trade and contact between the nomads of the Southern Atbai and its neighboring state, and any negative evidence for conflict between the two will enhance the argument in favor of the symbiotic model. As will be shown below, the Hagiz Group of the Taka phase fits all the above requirements.

The Evolution of Nomadism in the Southern Atbai

For ease of reference, the Southern Atbai cultural phases—the early, middle, and late Kassala Phase and the Taka Phase—will respectively be referred to as periods 1 through 4. The developmental trajectory to nomadism in the Southern Atbai is initially documented in four aspects of the data: geographic distribution of settlements, direct subsistence indicators from each period, and settlement patterns which indicate increasing population dispersal and mobility.

Geographic Distribution of Sites

In agreement with the symbiotic model, in period 1 sites were located along the Atbara and the paleo-Gash Rivers (Fig. 4.1a). Period 2 sites were also located in river valleys, but now along the Gash and its more recent channels swinging northward (Fig. 4.1b). By period 3, populations had expanded also into the hinterlands (Fig. 4.1c), a distribution similar to that of period 4, when, in addition, the Atbara river valley became occupied again (Fig. 4.1d).

Direct Subsistence Indicators

Faunal remains show that the period 1 populations pursued a mixed economy. Their subsistence strategy strongly relied on the hunting of a wide range of small and medium sized animals (Table App. 2.3). In the deposits of the later half of this period—that is to say, in the upper levels of the main sites such as KG 23 and 7, and in sites KG 96, 29 N and 5—bones of domesticated cattle, goats, and sheep are found. Characteristic stone picks of period 1, which appear to have been used for ground-breaking (Shiner 1971a; Steven M'Butu, personal communication), suggest that cultivation was also practiced. The use of wild and possibly domesticated plants is also documented by abundant grinding stones, and more directly by sorghum and millet seeds found embedded in period 1 sherds.

The direct subsistence indicators of period 2 suggest a similarly mixed economy. However, the faunal and macro-botanical sample from this period may not be representative as it all comes from the site of Mahal Teglinos. Small and large wild game and rodents are found throughout the two meters of stratified deposits at this site. Small and large riverine fauna are found in the upper levels only, perhaps indicating the time when the Gash River finally reached its present bed some 4 km west of Mahal Teglinos. Also found only in the upper layers are remains of domesticated cattle, goats, and sheep (Geraads 1983). Cultivation is indicated by numerous grinding stones, grinding holes in bedrock, clay lined storage pits, and actual seeds or imprints of *Hordeum* sp., *Ziziphus* sp., and *leguminosae* (Costantini et al. 1983).

In period 3, as evidence from two of the Mokram Group sites in the eastern steppe shows (KG 124, KG 20), the faunal list had become more

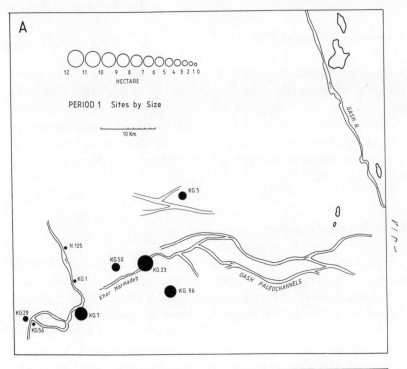

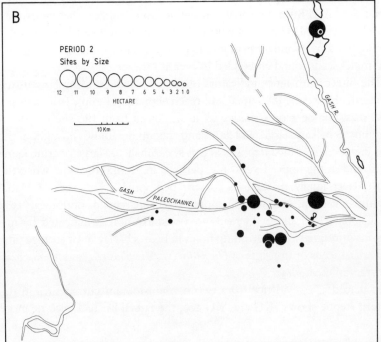

Figure 4.1. Distribution of sites. a) period 1; b) period 2.

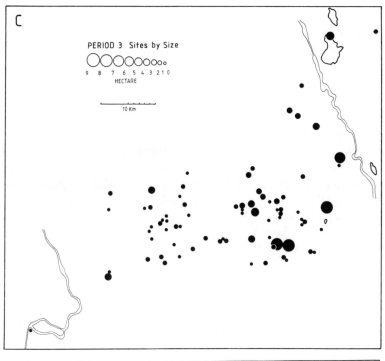

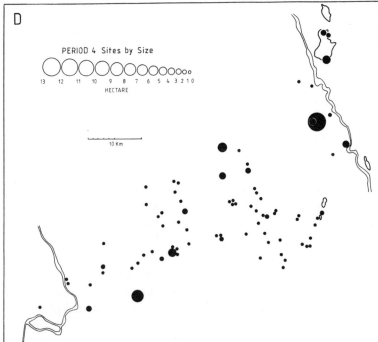

Figure 4.1. Distribution of sites. c) period 3; d) period 4.

limited. Fewer wild game were hunted, while fish remains are absent (Table App. 4.2). The domesticated fauna included cattle, goats, and sheep (Peters 1986). Two other period 3 sites near the Gash River (JAG 1, SEG 9) contained seeds and imprints of domesticated sorghum (Costantini et al. 1983). As expected, numerous grinding stones are present on all sites of this period.

The period 4 faunal remains—known from only one site—belong predominantly to cattle (Peters 1986). No macro-botanical remains have been recovered, and grinding stones—unlike the situation in all three preceding periods—are extremely rare (Table App. 5.2). The negative indication for cultivation and positive indication for pastoralism suggest the latter was more important in the period 4 economy.

Population Dispersal

As Table 4.1 shows, there was a gradual trend toward more population dispersal, as measured by a decrease in number of very large sites and an increase in the percentage of small sites from periods' 1 to 4. Although, as the ethnographic cases in chapter 2 showed, not all dispersed populations can be necessarily considered more pastoral in the northeast African setting, it remains true that all nomadic pastoralists tend toward a more dispersed settlement pattern.

Population Mobility

There are also indications that a progressively larger segment of the population was becoming mobile during the same time. This is indicated by a comparison of durations of occupation at each site during the four periods (Table 4.2). Durations of occupation are assessed from the depth of deposits and from surface artifact densities, as described in chapter 2. In period 1 most sites were not only large, but also had significant depths of deposits (between 1/2 and 2 m) and very high surface artifact densities. A few large and deep sites are also known from periods 2 and 3, but the majority were of medium density. In stark contrast, the vast majority of period 4 sites were low density. Since low density sites represent very short duration of occupation, one can conclude that the population of period 4 was highly mobile.

Table 4.1 Sites by Size, Periods 1–4.

Site size (ha)	Period 1		Period 2		Period 3		Period 4	
	n	%	n	%	n	%	n	%
0–1.9	3	33.3	20	66.6	61	75.3	59	83.0
2–3.9	1	11.1	5	16.6	14	17.2	7	9.8
4–5.9	2	22.2	0	0.0	2	2.4	3	4.2
6–7.9	1	11.1	2	6.6	3	3.7	1	1.4
8–9.9	1	11.1	1	3.3	1	1.2	0	0.0
10 +	1	11.1	2	6.6	0	0.0	1	1.4
Total	9	99.9	30	99.7	81	99.8	71	99.8

Other Evidence

The cumulative evidence so far shows that by period 4 a highly mobile, dispersed, predominantly pastoral population inhabited the study area. Their site proxemics provides additional evidence of their strongly pastoral orientation (Fig. 4.2).

There are two main clusters of period 4 sites, one in the eastern and the other in the western half of the study area. Each cluster has a large settlement nearer the river (KG III and K 16). In the eastern cluster, the greatest densities of the small sites occur between 15 and 20 km from the largest site. In the western cluster, highest densities occur 10–20 km away. This pattern brings to mind one associated with modern Sudanese herders (chapter 2): namely, that herds taken out beyond half a day's walk from the base (ca. 15–20 km) must be sheltered overnight in temporary herd camps. The period 4 pattern suggests just such an arrangment, with a large, perhaps seasonally

Table 4.2 Sites by Density, Periods 1–4.

Site density	Period 1		Period 2		Period 3		Period 4	
	n	%	n	%	n	%	n	%
High	7	77.7	3	10.7	2	2.5	0	0.0
Medium	0	0.0	18	64.2	44	55.0	3	4.2
Low	2	22.2	7	25.0	34	42.5	68	95.7
Total	9	99.9	28*	99.9	80*	100	71	99.9

*Site totals differ from those in Table 4.1 as artifact densities on a few sites were not recorded.

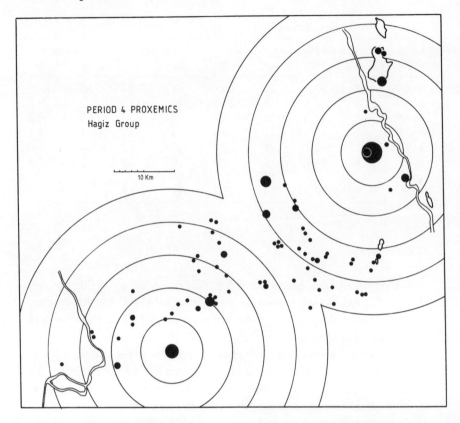

Figure 4.2. Period 4 site proxemics.

reoccupied riverside base and a ring of satellite herding camps.[1] The question which remains is whether the Hagiz Group sites represent a nomadic regional population, or the pastoral segment of a larger agropastoral regional population.

The answer to this lies in the period 4 site distribution against the land use zones of the Southern Atbai. During periods 1 and 2, sites were distributed near the main rivers, in what is presumed to have been then, as now, the most fertile parts of the study area. During periods 3 and 4, sites expanded outside the riverine zones. Assuming, as paleo-environmental reconstruction indicates, that during these later periods (ca. 1500 BC–AD 350) the land use zones of the area resembled those of today, it is interesting

Table 4.3 Comparison of Period 3 and 4 Site Distributions by Land Use Zones

Land use zones	Period 3 sites		Period 4 sites	
	n	%	n	%
Within 5 km of primary agricultural lands	6	7.3	9	12.6
Within 5 km of secondary agricultural lands	29	35.3	18	25.3
Within 5 km of tertiary agricultural lands	27	32.9	28	39.4
Marginal lands	20	24.4	16	22.5
Total	82	99.9	71	99.8

to note the strong similarity in site distributions of periods 3 and 4 (Table 4.3). These are practically identical, in spite of the fact that the period 4 populations apparently were specialized herders, while those of period 3, as will be shown below, were agropastoralists.

Since during period 4 the predominantly pastoral Hagiz Group population inhabited even the best agricultural lands of the study area, it is unlikely that they were simply the herding segment of a regional agropastoral population. Considering that today (probably as in period 4) the Kassala area agricultural lands are the most fertile in the eastern Sudan (Barbour 1964), nowhere else in the region could the agricultural sections of a hypothetically agropastoral Hagiz Group pursue intensive agriculture. The Hagiz population of period 4 Southern Atbai are thus most reasonably interpreted as true nomads.

True agropastoralists, on the other hand, seem to have inhabited the study area in the previous period. From period 3 almost half the surveyed sites have associated earthen mounds which have been interpreted as animal corrals (Table App. 4.3). These features are circular 10–20 m in diameter, up to 60 cm tall, and with a raised lip at the edge (Fig. 4.3). They are sometimes located in the center of a site, at other times off to the side. There are never any artifacts atop these features, nor did the one test pit excavated in one of the mounds recover any more than a few period 3 sherds.

Initially these circular features were thought to be the remains of well pools (Sadr 1983), but their distribution was later found not to correlate with the underground hydrography of the area. Subsequently they were thought to be the remains of house mounds (Sadr 1986), but there is usually only one feature associated with a site, no matter how big the site. Indeed the biggest sites have none of these features. Since the features are found

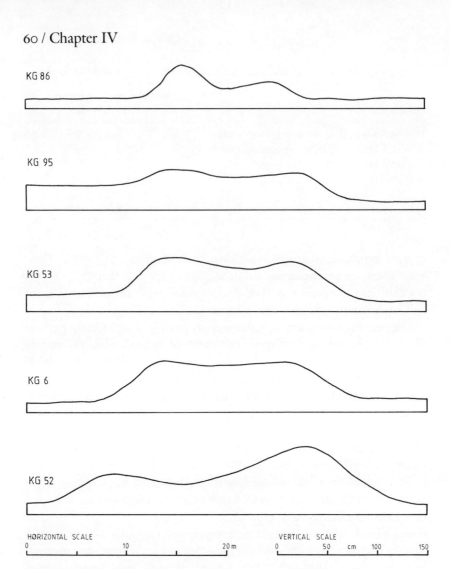

Figure 4.3. Five earthen mounds in section (vertical exaggeration 10:1).

mostly in the more marginal zones, a function associated with herding seems most likely; perhaps they were built to keep the cattle's hooves dry in the rainy season when the clay plains of the Southern Atbai turn into a sea of mud (such may have been necessary to avoid certain hoof diseases, cf., e.g., Evans-Pritchard 1940: 57).

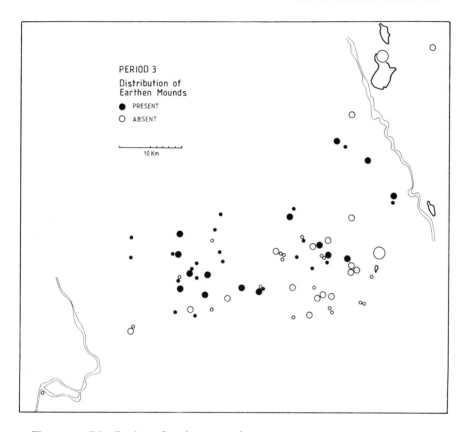

Figure 4.4. Distribution of earthen mounds.

In fact, the distribution of period 3 earthen features somewhat matches the base/satellite herding camp pattern seen in the period 4 proxemics. One site—K 10, located along the Gash—contains six of these earthen mounds. Most other sites contain only one, a few have two. The farther west from the Gash River, the more of these mounds are encountered (Fig.4.4). As in period 4, in the concentric circles around K 10 a cluster of mounds are in a band 10–20 km away, and another in a band 25–35 km away. The latter may again represent a different cluster of satellite herding camps centered on an as yet unknown K 10-like site nearer the Atbara river valley. The data may indicate the base/satellite dispersion of a herding segment within the period 3 population.

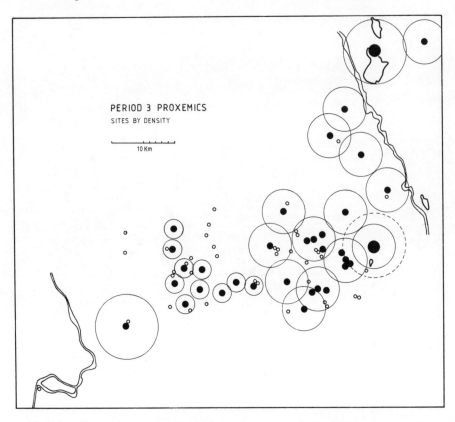

Figure 4.5. Period 3 site proxemics (Late Mokram sites not included).

Two other possible segments emerge in the period 3 settlement patterns if one looks at other aspects of the site proxemics (Fig. 4.5). There is a clear boundary between the sites of the eastern and the western steppe. In the eastern steppe, the nearest-neighbor distances of medium and high density sites[2] are distributed fairly evenly at an average distance of 6.86 km from each other.[3] In the western steppe, on the other hand, the average distance separating medium density sites is only about 3.4 km, or 4.38 km if one includes the outlier KG 20.

Considering the pattern of smaller site catchments in the more arid and less arable western half of the study area, one interpretation is that the western sites were not as agriculturally oriented as those in the east; if they

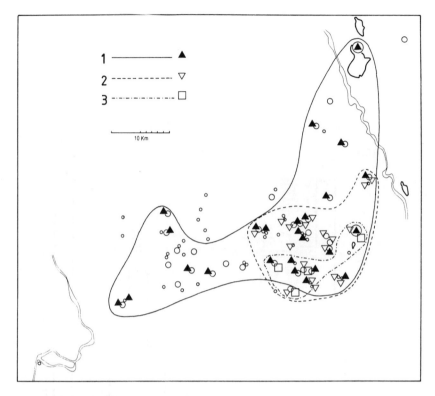

Figure 4.6. Distribution of three period 3 ceramic markers. Marker 1) zig-zag rim top relief decoration (see Figure 5.1e); marker 2) single-row punctation rim band decoration; marker 3) mat-impressed body decoration (Late Mokram characteristic).

were, they should have had larger catchments than in the east. In this light it may also be significant that the macro-botanical evidence for period 3 sorghum was found in sites of the eastern steppe.

What the period 3 proxemic patterns possibly indicate is the presence of separate economic sectors within the same regional population. That these segments may represent sub-regional populations like the modern ethnographically known clans is perhaps suggested by some minor stylistic boundaries visible in the ceramic distributions (Fig. 4.6). In support is also the geographic scale of the period 3 segments, which fit comfortably within the range of ethnographically recorded segments among modern pastoralist populations (Fig. 4.7). Thus, overall, the available evidence allows an interpretation of agropastoralism during period 3.

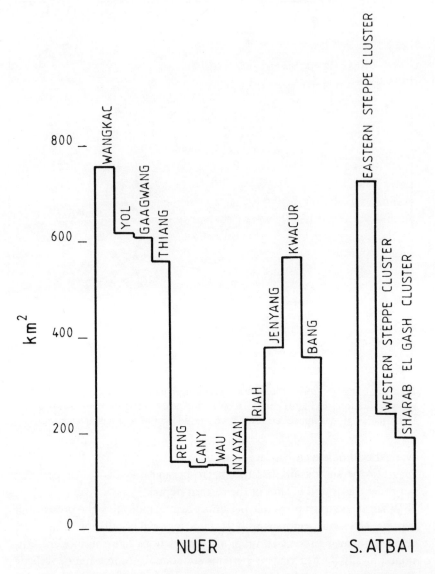

Figure 4.7. Comparison of Nuer section sizes (after Evans-Pritchard 1940) to possible section areas in the Southern Atbai.

Social Complexity

The sequence of change in Southern Atbai adaptive strategies apparently follows the path predicted by the symbiotic model, at least insofar as a mixed economy adaptation was transformed into an agropastoral one and finally into a fully nomadic one. It follows the predicted path also in that there was parallel development in social, political, and economic complexity.

The available data indicate that the population of period 1 was fairly egalitarian. Five of the eight sites of this period were long term village settlements; of the others, two were small homestead-size settlements, and another was a small, short term camp settlement. There is no indication of administrative site hierarchy, or inter-site differences in wealth as measured by the quality of material remains and the presence of exotic goods. The one burial which was encountered in the BAP excavations at KG 23 (intrusive?) had no associated grave goods.

Socio-political complexity in early period 2 (known only from limited excavations in the lower strata of Mahal Teglinos) may have been similar to that of period 1. At least, there is yet no indication that it was significantly different.

In late period 2, however, the situation was definitely different. The site proxemics of the Gash Group (Fig. 4.8) show a very hierarchic site distribution with large, long term village settlements like JAG 1 forming the center to a constellation of smaller, medium term villages, hamlets, and homesteads: in other words, center and support population in hierarchic arrangement.[4] Clay seals have been found at Mahal Teglinos, which may match similar ones found at Kerma (an important trade center in Nubia, see chapter 7), and which attest to complex administrative functions (Fattovich, personal communication). In addition, elaborate grave superstructures with monolithic stelae (Fattovich 1989) have been found at this site, which may represent some mark of status differentiation.

Intersite differences in the distribution of unusually or exotically decorated ceramic vessels (Fig. 4.9, Table App. 3.3) may give an indication of disparities in wealth, or at least in the production and distribution of these exotics. In either case, the cumulative evidence suggests a chiefdom-like level of socio-political organization during the second half of period 2.

According to the symbiotic model, an agropastoral adaptation could appear in period 2. In reality, this cannot be documented. The survey seems

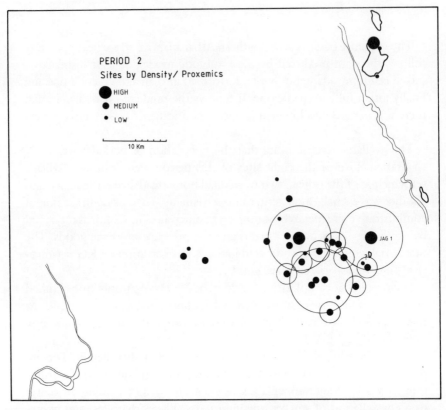

Figure 4.8. Proxemics and distribution of Gash Group sites by surface artifact density.

to catch just a small corner of the territory of the period 2 Gash Group population; the size of the known period 2 population in the study area is no larger than a typical segment, so inter-segmental specialization cannot be documented even if it existed. Gash Group-like ceramics found at Agordat (Arkell 1954), and monolithic stelae near Aqiq on the Red Sea coast (Fattovich 1989) suggest that the regional distribution of the period 2 population may have extended considerably east and northeast of the study area. Whether a pastoral segment of the Gash Group operated there remains unknown.

By period 3, however, an agropastoral population seems securely documented in the study area. Socio-politically, period 3 seems to have been

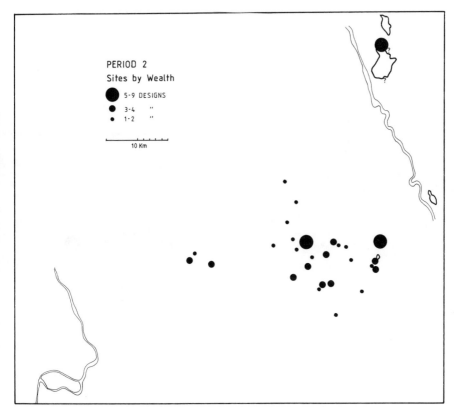

Figure 4.9. Distribution of Gash Group sites by "wealth."

more or less as complex as period 2, although the data are more limited. The period 3 exotic ceramic distributions (Fig. 4.10, and Table App. 4. 5) show a similarly biased pattern. The settlement distribution of period 3 by density (Fig. 4.5), no less orderly than that of period 2, does not display the center/satellite hierarchy as clearly. Nevertheless, in rank size distribution, the period 2 and 3 sites are almost identical.

Figure 4.11 shows a combination of the data from Tables 4.1 and 4.2 in graph form. Site sizes have been weighted with their duration of occupation in such a way that high density sites are calculated for three times their size, medium density sites for their size doubled, and low density sites by size alone (Mahal Teglinos is thus counted in at 11 ha $\times$ 3 = 33 ha/density

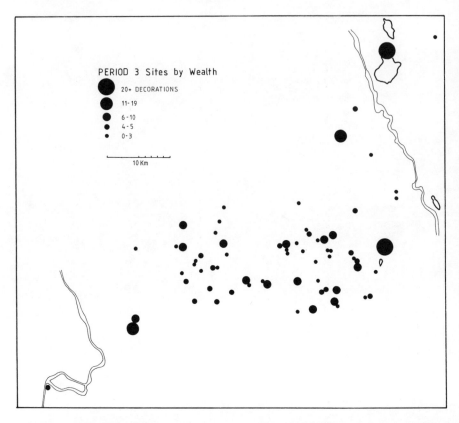

Figure 4.10. Distribution of period 3 sites by "wealth." Late Mokram sites not included.

units). In this way two sites of similar size but different durations of occupation (e.g., one seasonal, the other long term) will have their rank appropriately adjusted. As the figure shows, period 2 and 3 rank/size distributions are more similar than either is to those of periods 1 and 4. Thus, the expected correlation between agropastoralism and chiefdom-like ranked social organization seems confirmed.

A final point of agreement between the Southern Atbai sequence and the symbiosis model is encountered in the final period. Although the Taka Phase is rather poorly dated (see chapter 3), nomadism seems to have emerged in the Southern Atbai more or less at the same time as the Kushitic and the pre-Axumite kingdoms appeared in the neighboring regions. Judging by the textually known interactions between these states and some of

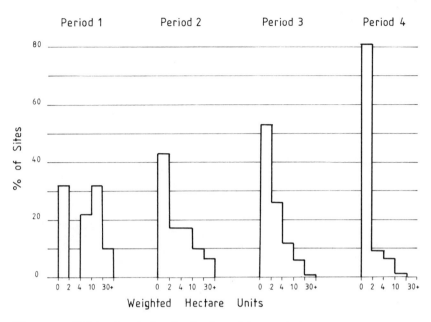

Figure 4.11. Weighted rank size distribution of sites, periods 1–4.

their nomadic neighbors (as will be discussed in more detail in chapter 8), the Southern Atbai nomads of period 4 were in a good position to benefit from nomad/sedentary symbiotic relations with these states. Alas, there is little hope of finding direct evidence for trade in agricultural and pastoral products, but the pre-Axumite ceramics found on Hagiz Group sites (Fattovich, Marks, and Mohammed-Ali 1984) at least serve to indicate that the two were in contact.

In sum, the picture archaeologically presented closely resembles the hypothetical symbiosis model trajectory of change. Unfortunately, however, the data remain too coarse-grained to show the actual event of transformation from period 3 agropastoralism to period 4 nomadism.

What little is known suggests that the late Mokram Group population abandoned the immediate surroundings of Jebel Kassala and the western steppe (Fig. 4.12). The late Mokram Group medium density sites are found in the southern Sharab, surrounded to the north and west by a ring of low density sites. Three isolated low density sites are scattered farther. To the south of the Sharab, a 10 km long survey transect failed to locate any other Late Mokram Group sites.

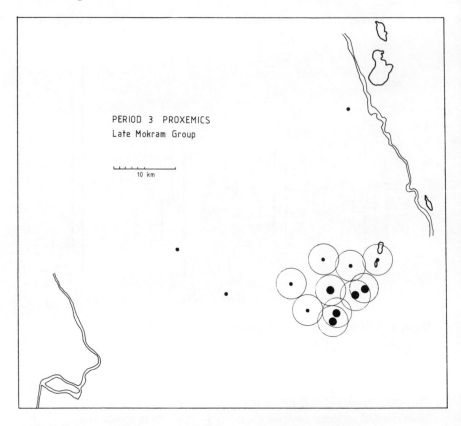

PERIOD 3 PROXEMICS
Late Mokram Group

10 km

Figure 4.12. Late Mokram Group proxemics against sites by density.

The cluster in the Sharab can be interpreted by its small scale as a mixed economy population. But there is no indication whether it was a segment of a larger agropastoral regional population, or a part of a regionally mixed economy one.

In general, the late period 3 remains seem an impoverished relic of the classic Mokram Group. The ceramics are of poorer quality with a signifi-cant proportion fiber tempered, and the range in decorations is much more limited (Sadr, ms.). Possibly, if Fattovich (1985) is correct in his identifica-tion of the Kassala area as part of Punt (chapter 3), the impoverishment began around 1100 BC with the cessation of trade with Egypt (see chapter 7). The Southern Atbai apparently became a political and economic hinterland, and eventually, by around 750 BC, the local population turned to a nomadic way of life.[5]

There is no evidence for any conflict between the Southern Atbai and the rising states to its east and west, nor any indication that the climate deteriorated in the early first millennium BC. There is no information on the state/hinterland relations during this time to indicate precisely how the interactions with the neighboring states affected the Southern Atbai population. Thus, there is no information on the initial "kick" which sent the population into nomadism. Nevertheless, as the above discussions have shown, environmental factors can hardly have played a role, since the Hagiz nomads were the sole occupants of the fertile Kassala area. Conflict is likewise unlikely: there is some information (chapter 8) that warfare spelled the end of nomadism in the Southern Atbai around AD 350.

Now, what about the areas beyond the Southern Atbai? Does the symbiosis model fit any other cases of nomadism developing in ancient Egypt, Sudan, and Ethiopia, or does the Southern Atbai sequence represent an anomalous case? The next chapter sets the stage for a reexamination of the four known separate sequences to nomadism in northeast Africa.

Chapter V
Nomads in Ancient Northeast Africa

Introduction

The ancient nomads of Egypt, northern Sudan, and northern Ethiopia are very poorly represented in the archaeological record for two related reasons: first, because the spectacular remains in the Nile Valley vastly outshine the decidedly unspectacular remains in the hinterlands; and, second, because formidable logistical hurdles are inherent in running an archaeological expedition in the inhospitable hinterlands.

In contrast to the paucity of research in the hinterlands, up to the second World War the Egyptian and northern Sudanese Nile Valley (Fig. 5.1) were archaeologically investigated by such illustrious figures as Lepsius, Reisner, Firth, Woolley, McIver, Emery, and Kirwan, among many others (Trigger 1976). In the early 1960s, an international effort to rescue archaeological remains from the waters of Lake Nasser brought to light a wealth of information on ancient Nubian cultures. Ever since, research has continued in the Nile Valley, but work in the hinterlands has been restricted to the ongoing projects of Wendorf (et al. 1980, 1984) and Kuper (1981, 1986) to the west of the Nile. This picture may now change with the start of investigations by Italian, German, and American teams in the deserts east of the Nile and on the Red Sea coast. As yet, however, vast regions in the hinterlands remain archaeologically unknown.

Farther south, in the Upper Nubian Nile Valley, research has been restricted to the sites of Kerma (Bonnet et al. 1982, 1984, 1986; Reisner 1923) and Jebel Barkal (Donadoni 1983; Reisner 1917), and some surveys by the French Archaeological Unit of the Sudanese Antiquities Service (Villa 1975–1984; Reinold 1987), as well as others carried out by Shiner in the late sixties (Shiner 1971b).

In the Middle Nile the picture is less bleak. Many individuals and projects—Sudanese, French, Italian, English, German, American, and Polish teams (Mohammed-Ali 1982; Geus 1976, 1977, 1980, 1982, 1986; Reinold 1987; Lenoble 1987; Caneva 1988; Arkell 1949, 1953; Shinnie 1967; Krzyzaniak 1977b) among others—have worked on the rich Mesolithic, Neolithic, and Meroitic remains. Even in the hinterlands of the Middle Nile,

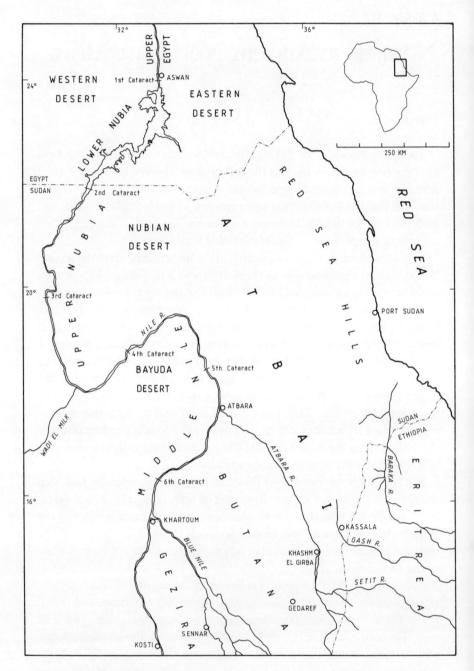

Figure 5.1. Northeast Africa.

especially in the Butana grasslands, investigators have ventured far (Marks et al. 1985; Hintze 1959).

Elsewhere in the Sudan, serious research has been restricted to a couple of sites in the Gezira, south of Khartoum (Addison 1949, 1956), and in the Kassala area of the eastern Sudan where the combined efforts of the BAP and the IAMSK have unearthed, among other data, the information presented in previous chapters.

Farther east, the highlands of northern Ethiopia have been the subject of archaeological investigation since the early years of this century (Littman 1913; Puglisi 1941; Anfray 1965, 1972). Here again, however, the spectacular remains of the Axumite and pre-Axumite kingdoms of the first millennia BC and AD have overshadowed research on the less spectacular earlier remains in the area,which, except for Arkell's (1954) work at Agordat and Dombrowski's (1972) in Begmeder, remain practically unknown.

The paucity of direct archaeological information on ancient nomads in northeast Africa is offset to a large degree by the information contained in ancient texts, which often allude to nomadic populations, to their location and relation with the states which left the records. These texts, along with what scattered archaeological data are available provide enough evidence for at least a preliminary investigation into the development of nomadism across this part of the continent.

The combined information available allows the reconstruction of four major sequences of transition to nomadism in separate areas of northeast Africa and at different times in its prehistoric record. Of these, one includes the Southern Atbai sequence described in the previous chapter; another concerns Upper Egypt from about 4500–3000 BC; a third involves Nubia from about 2500–1000 BC; and the final sequence deals with Nubia between the first and fifth centuries AD. These four sequences are discussed one by one in the chapters ahead.

Before moving on, however, a word or two on the identification of nomads and other pastoral populations in the various sequences. The methods used in chapter 4 cannot all be applied to the northeast African sequences because large scale surveys of the kind designed to distinguish between pastoral types have not been attempted except in the Southern Atbai. This is not a major hindrance to identifying mixed economy and fully agricultural populations, but nomads and agropastoralists cannot be properly documented without such surveys (see chapter 2). Of necessity, therefore, the analyses in the following chapters have to rely strongly on circumstantial evidence. The kinds of evidence used vary from place to place and time to time, so a general description of methods cannot be given. Instead, the lines of evidence used will be made explicit at the appropriate juncture.

Because the testing of the symbiotic model also requires that the level of socio-political complexity of each archaeological culture be known, it is appropriate to briefly discuss methods of determining these, as well. The society's level of complexity in political, economic, and social structures (Service 1975; Claessen 1981) is often best seen in mortuary practices, in inequalities of wealth and status among individuals in a society as reflected by the richness of materials with which the individuals were interred. Luckily, burials have received a disproportionate amount of attention in northeast African archaeology, so data on this aspect of each society are abundant. Other factors such as public architecture, artifacts reflecting administrative duties and so forth are also used when appropriate. Again, no general rules of identification will be presented. Instead each case will be discussed individually in the next four chapters.

Finally, the question of how the sequence is divided into discrete regional and temporal archaeological cultures and their phases (Fig. 5.2) must be briefly discussed. The divisions used are those presented by the principal investigators of each region, and all original nomenclature—such as Kerma culture, C-Group, Karat industry—have been retained. These archaeological cultures are often subdivided into phases, which are likewise retained in the following discussions. The dating for each such phase and references to primary sources are provided in the text.

The gross geographical subdivisions of northeast Africa follow ecologically significant boundaries which apparently were also culturally significant. Roughly, these are the Upper Egyptian Nile Valley, the Nile Valley of Lower Nubia, Upper Nubia, and the Middle Nile. The Nile here is essentially an elongated oasis, in the north with wide and in the south with narrower alluvial floodplains, which is bounded to the east and west by arid deserts in Upper Egypt and Lower and Upper Nubia, and, south of the 17th parallel, by the less arid savannas of the Butana and the Gezira. The savanna of the Southern Atbai, to the east, was described earlier (chapter 3). Farther east, the highlands of northern Ethiopia differ significantly from the Sudanese and Egyptian lowlands, being more fertile and well watered. As there is little direct archaeological information from the deserts east and west of the Nile, the Butana grasslands, and the northern Ethio-Sudanese border-

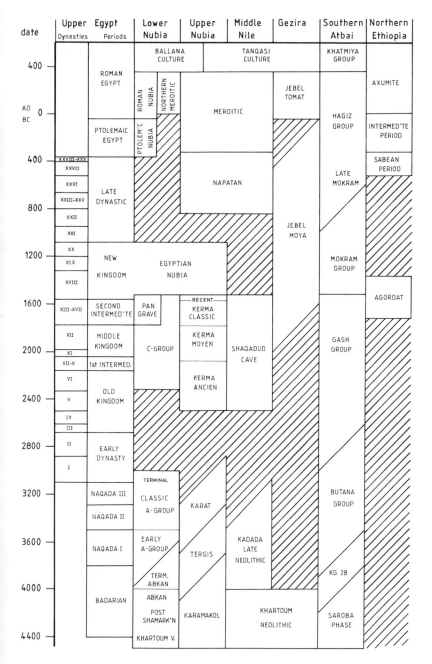

Figure 5.2. Northeast African archaeological sequences.

lands, they have been left out of Figure 5.2: their ancient inhabitants are better known from texts.

The stage is thus set for a presentation of the first trajectory toward a fully nomadic adaptation in the Upper Egyptian and Nubian regions of the study area during the fifth and fourth millennia BC.

Chapter VI

Nomads on the Fringe of the Developing Pharaonic State

Egypt and Nubia, 4500–3000 BC

The events described below touch on developments in the Egyptian and Nubian Nile Valleys and their eastern and western hinterlands during the second half of the fifth and the entire fourth millennia BC (Fig. 6.1). The period covers the Neolithic humid phase as defined by Muzzolini (1982). The Saharan lakes at Adrar Bous, Chad, and Tibesti were at a high level (A.B. Smith 1976; Courtin 1966; Servant and Servant-Vildary 1980; Pachur 1975; Jäkel 1978). In the eastern Sahara, at the beginning of this period, vegetation zones were 300–400 km north of their present positions (Neumann 1989), while in the western Sudan the rainfall belts between 4000 and 3000 BC were about 100 km north of present positions (Warren 1970). The accumulation of the Kibdi formation in Upper Egypt (Butzer 1975) and the Playa II at Nabta (Wendorf and Schild 1980) also provide evidence for this wet phase. The end of this period, however, may have witnessed a gradual trend toward aridity (Hoffman et al. 1986). Below, the archaeological sequence of this period is described by region in three phases; the early part 4500–4000 BC, the middle part from 4000–3500 BC, and the late part from 3500–3000 BC.

4500–4000 BC (Fig. 6.2)

The few known sites from the early part of this period suggest that mixed economies were the order of the day. The Badarian population of Upper Egypt, for example, known from a few sites near Asyut of 4400–4000 BC (Hassan 1985), pursued an economy which left remains of cereals, wild plant foods, domesticated cattle and small livestock, hunted animals, fish, and fowl on their sites (Brunton and Caton-Thompson 1928; Brunton 1932, 1937, 1947; Mond and Myers 1937; Kaiser 1961; Hays 1976; Fairservice 1972). Their sites, located both in the alluvial zone and in the bordering terraces

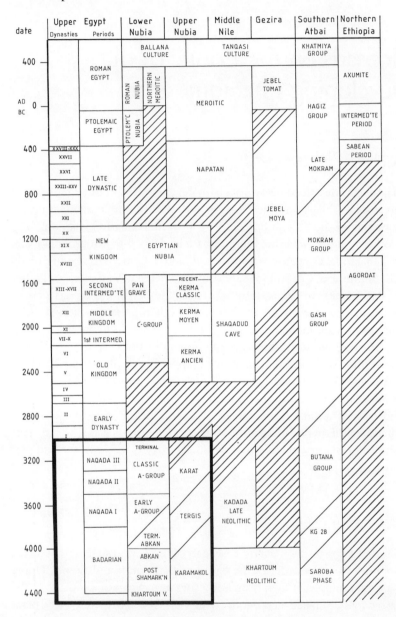

Figure 6.1. Egypt and Nubia, 4500–3000 BC.

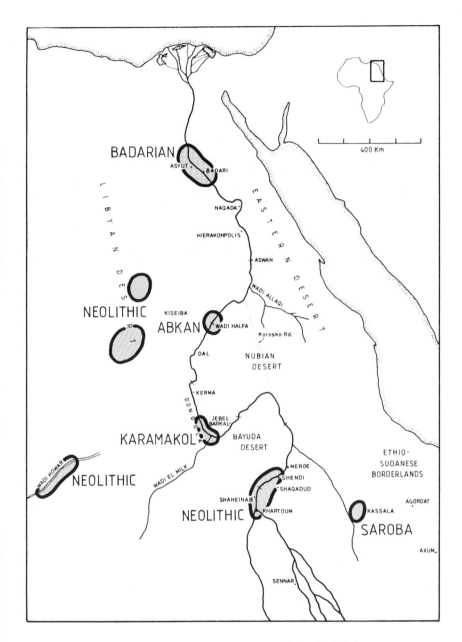

Figure 6.2. Northeast Africa, 4500–4000 BC. Lightly shaded forms represent mixed economy regional populations.

may have been occupied in different seasons for different subsistence activities. Fattovich (1984) compares their settlement system to the modern Nuer's.

Farther up the Nile, during the same period, three apparently consecutive Lower Nubian archaeological cultures seem to have pursued a mixed economy. The Khartoum Variant (Shiner 1968a), represented by eight small sites near Wadi Halfa, is not securely dated, but ceramic affinities with the Middle Nile Khartoum Neolithic suggest a fifth millennium BC date (Nordström 1972). One of the sites (CPE 2016) had an in situ mud plaster floor and quantities of burnt rock (Shiner 1968 a). This floor, and the deep deposits on this site, as well as high surface artifact densities at all of the Khartoum Variant sites—even those located 15 km from the Nile (Shiner 1968a; Nordström 1972)—suggest fairly stable, long term occupations by a relatively sedentary population. Although only bones of fish and some molluscs have been found associated with the riverside sites, the presence of many formal tools in the lithic industry (Shiner 1968a) suggests that hunting was also pursued. The overall picture suggests a mixed economic adaptation, albeit perhaps one without any domesticated plants or animals.

The Abkan can also be reasonably identified as a mixed economy population. Represented by nearly twenty sites in the vicinity of Wadi Halfa—one of which is dated to the late fifth millennium BC (Nordström 1972)—the Abkan adaptation seems to have focused on fishing, supplemented by hunting and gathering. The sites are located along the Nile in areas suitable for positioning fish traps (Shiner 1968b). A possible rock drawing of one such trap (Myers 1958), and large numbers of fish remains are associated with these sites (e.g., as at site 5-3-25, Adams and Nordström 1963). Also, a variety of hunted animals, including gazelle, equids, large bovids, and geese, as well as grinding stones are found on most sites (Nordström 1972; Shiner 1968b). As in the Khartoum variant case, the Abkan mixed economy adaptation may not have included use of domesticated plants and animals.

Some of the Abkan sites, such as Myers's (1960) Abka IX, have in situ deposits (also Carlson 1966), while another, site 6-G-25, contained numerous fragments of burnt, well oxidized clay which may originally have been parts of huts or ovens (Nordström 1972). The sites set close to the river edge, which would have been subject to flooding, may have been seasonal fishing camps (Nordström 1972). Seasonal mobility may also be indicated by the range in the size of sites from a few hectares to only 100 m² (e.g., CPE 629 and 604, as opposed to CPE 1029, Shiner 1968b), a situation which can suggest either base and satellite camps, or seasonal nucleation and dispersal of the population.

The evidence for the post Shamarkian, and the Karamakol Group of Upper Nubia is not complete enough to allow identification of adaptation. Faunal remains are absent on all nine sites which make up the material inventory of these two poorly known, separate regional groups (Schild et al. 1968; Nordström 1972; Hays 1971a). All sites are small and located along the Nile, and most contain ceramics, lithics, and groundstones. Despite the lack of data, what remains there are suggest a mixed economy population more than any of the other three types of pastoral adaptation.

Considering that the contemporaneous Khartoum Neolithic of the Middle Nile—especially as seen in the remains at Geili (Caneva 1985a,b), Esh Shaheinab (Arkell 1953), Kadero I (Haaland 1981; Krzyzaniak 1977b), and Shaqadud (Marks et al. 1985)—represents a sedentary or semi-sedentary mixed economy population, as does the Malawiya Group of the Southern Atbai (Marks and Sadr 1988; Fattovich, Marks, and Mohammed-Ali 1984), it seems that all riverine settings of northeast Africa during the second half of the fifth millennium BC were occupied by populations following basically similar mixed economy strategies, which in some cases included cultivation of domesticated plants, and herding of domesticated animals. Settlement patterns generally included small, semi-permanent or permanent base camp occupations, with related short term satellite camps at which seasonally specific tasks may have been carried out (Haaland 1981; Sadr 1986). Only in the Khartoum Neolithic sites, with the predominance of cattle at Kadero, is there the barest hint of inter-site specialization in subsistence activity during this time (Krzyzaniak 1977b).

Some regions have not yielded any secure evidence for occupation during this time. In northern Ethiopia, for example, some very poorly known micro- and macrolithic industries may date to this time (Philipson 1977; Clark 1970; Fattovich 1984 d), but little is known about their adaptation. In the western hinterlands of the Nile, however, in Wadi Howar and even farther west in Adrar Bous, mixed economy populations are documented and dated roughly to the early and middle part of this period, ca. 4500–3500 BC.

In the western Sudan, sites have been found along the Wadi Howar (Mohammed-Ali 1982; Kuper 1986), which, although not securely dated, can on artifactual grounds be assigned to the fourth and third millennia BC (ibid.). Most likely, they date to the Neolithic humid phase. Some of the sites, although small, have up to 30 cm depth of deposits (UMB-4, Mohammed Ali 1982), suggesting stable, relatively long term occupation. Other sites are widely scattered. Farther north, similar evidence suggests similar mixed economy societies in southwest Egypt (Hahn 1988), near Abu Ballas (Kuper 1988) and on the Selima Sandsheet (Schuck 1988).

A mixed economy subsistence with reliance on domesticated animals is also documented from areas farther west in sites of the Tenerian Culture (A.B. Smith 1980). There, the populations of earlier times had lived in lakeside settlements, subsisting on hunting, gathering, and fishing. With the acquisition of domesticated cattle and perhaps domesticated plants, a semi-sedentary life continued around the same Saharan lakes. At Agorass-in-Tast numerous large and small rock circles—which have been interpreted as hut bases and the bases for grain bins (Clark et al. 1973)—as well as the high density of artifacts (including grinding stones), and the presence of some in situ deposits below the surface suggest a semi-permanent base camp occupation.

4000–3500 BC (Fig. 6.3)

Except in Upper Egypt, adaptations in the Nile Valley during this period are less well documented. The Post-Shamarkian and Khartoum Variant industries were replaced by the Early A-Group in the northern parts of Lower Nubia, between Kubania and Sayala (Nordström 1972). Cross-dating places the Early A-Group between 4000 and 3500 BC (Trigger 1965; Nordström 1972). Trigger (1965) interprets the only known habitation site as a semi-permanent settlement. Faunal remains are rare, but at Khor Bahan include domesticated animals (Reisner 1910). Early A-Group graves near the river suggest that the population was based in the valley itself: probably they followed a mixed economy strategy, but there is not enough data to substantiate this claim.

In southern Lower Nubia, by the Second Cataract, the radiocarbon dated Terminal Abkan is known from only four sites (Nordström 1972). As far as can be judged, adaptations remained comparable to those of the preceding Developed Abkan industry.

In the Dongola reach of Upper Nubia, the Tergis industry, although undated, seems on artifactual grounds to follow upon the Karamakol industry (Hays 1971b). Lack of identifiable faunal remains in the five known

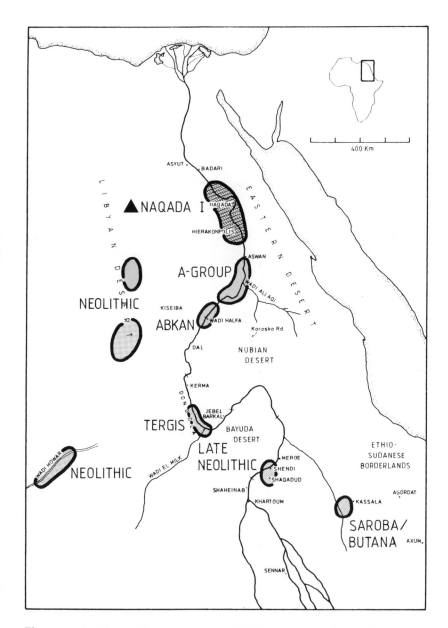

Figure 6.3. Northeast Africa, 4000–3500 BC. Dark gray, lightly pinstriped form represents agropastoral regional population. Small filled triangle preceding label denotes ranked (chiefdom) level of political organization. Absence of triangle denotes low level of socio-political complexity (egalitarian society). For explanation of other symbols see Figure 6.2.

Tergis sites makes it impossible to document a subsistence strategy. The sites are somewhat larger than those of the Karamakol, and have quite dense concentrations of surface artifacts: two sites (N 3 and N 55) contained some in situ materials. Pottery, lithics, and grinding stones were common; stone rings may indicate that some cultivation took place.

In the Middle Nile region, drastic demographic changes were occurring. After ca. 4000 BC the only known occupations in the Middle Nile Valley are found at Kadada, in the vicinity of Shendi. Similar materials have been recovered from graves at Kadruka near Kerma (Reinold 1987). Several dates from Kadada fall within the fourth millennium BC (Geus 1986). The material remains here are mostly from burials, although some occupation areas seem also to be present (Geus 1976–1982; 1986). Faunal remains include molluscs, fish, and reptiles, as well as wild and domesticated mammals (Gautier 1986). The evidence suggests that the broad range mixed economy subsistence strategy of the Khartoum Neolithic continued into the late Neolithic period, but in view of the paucity of remains little else can be said.

In contrast to the apparent continuity of mixed economies in most regions of northeast Africa, there are grounds for supposing that the population of the Upper Egyptian Nile Valley turned to a more specialized agropastoral adaptation after ca. 4000 BC.

The data are scant, but there are some significant clues. The Naqada I (Amratian) sites of Upper Egypt (dated to ca. 3800–3500 BC: Hoffman 1982; Hassan 1985) represent a further development of the base/satellite camp settlement patterns seen in the Badarian occupation (Hoffman 1982). Large sites located at the edge of the floodplain, such as Armant (Mond and Myers 1937), and Hierakonpolis (Hoffman et al. 1986) must have been the main population centers. Architectural remains at these towns include semi-subterranean and rectilinear houses (Hoffman et al. 1986). They also include extensive cemeteries where some large, rich Amratian tombs indicate social stratification at Hierakonpolis (Hoffman 1982).

The Hierakonpolis sites are internally diversified and were surrounded by smaller, more specialized satellite camps. These may have acted as seasonally specific centers for food procurement (notably herding and dry farming: Hoffman 1982, 1986). Some of the satellite sites were production centers for pottery, stone vessels, and beads (Butzer 1959; Hoffman 1982; Fattovich 1984). One small site, L 3, suggests that pastoral production was also a specialized activity. At this site, unlike the rectilinear and semi-subterranean houses found in Hierakonpolis, several round hut structures were uncovered. These,compared with remains at Hierakonpolis, suggest a "rural/urban" division of the population (Hoffman 1982), which may reflect specialization in economic activity of the kind attributable to an agropastoral population. Admittedly, the evidence is tenuous: surveys away from the Nile are imperative before the identification can be considered secure. If it stands, though, its occurrence in an economically, and presumably politically ranked society fits the conditions of the symbiosis model.

3500–3000 BC (Fig. 6.4)

After 3500 BC, in Egypt developments sped up considerably. The Late Predynastic (Naqada II, or Gerzean) was closely followed by the Terminal Predynastic (Naqada III, or Semainean), and by 3100 BC the dynastic history of Egypt had begun (Hoffman et al. 1986; Hassan 1985). Fattovich (1984) classifies the Naqada II society as a chiefdom, while Trigger (1965) and Hoffman et al. (1986) speak already of state society. Settlements during Naqada II became focused on the edge of the river alluvium (Hoffman 1982). Agricultural villages, as at Armant, Abydos, and Mahasna (Mond and Myers 1937; Peet 1914; Garstang 1903), and the South Town at Zawaydah (Fairservice 1972; Butzer 1959; Petrie 1896) were occupied. Hierakonpolis during this time had an urban population (Hoffman et al. 1986). There appear to have been some semi-permanent occupations at sites located some distance from the river (e.g., Hammamiya: Brunton and Caton-Thompson 1928; Trigger 1965), but in the vicinity of Hierakonpolis there was a noticeable shift away from desert-edge settlements into more nucleated sites in the agricultural zone of the Nile Valley (Hoffman et al. 1986).

Large and rich tumulus burials at the towns attest to the increasing stratification of society (Hofman et al 1986). Grain kilns found at Abydos and Mahasna indicate the importance of agriculture (Peet 1914; Garstang 1903), while the specialized production centers at such sites as Nag'Hammadi (Vignard 1920),Wadi el Sheikh (Morgan 1897), and others (Butzer 1974), and probable markets, as at the South Town (Petrie 1896; Baumgartel 1970; Fattovich 1984), give a good indication of the levels of commercial complexity achieved in Naqada II times. The trade contact of the Naqada II culture went as far as the Eastern and Western Deserts of Egypt, Nubia, and even the Near East (Hoffman 1982; Krzyzaniak 1977a; Fattovich 1984).

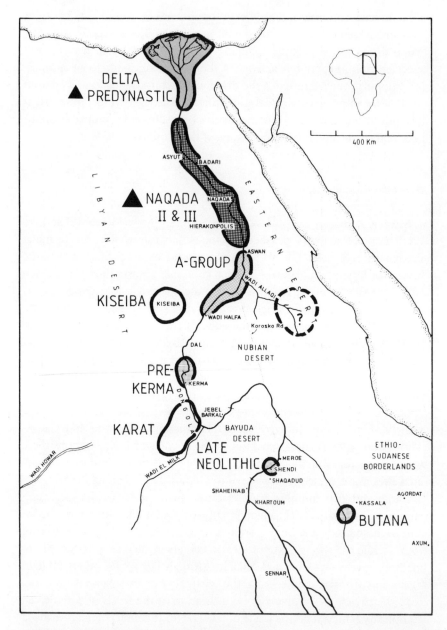

Figure 6.4. Northeast Africa, 3500–3000 BC. Darkest form represents agricultural regional population. Forms without shading represent nomadic regional populations. Large filled triangle preceding label represent state level of political organization. For explanation of other symbols see Figures 6.2 and 6.3.

The population shift toward agricultural villages in the alluvium continued, indeed increased, in Naqada III times (Hoffman et al. 1986). Irrigation appeared (Butzer 1976), and was controlled by such rulers as King Scorpion (Hoffman 1986). Wealth increased throughout all strata of society. At Nekhen and site L.25c(1) palace and temple structures have been provisionally identified (Hoffman 1982, Hoffman et al. 1986). Naqada III, with its capital at Hierakonpolis, can surely be described as an early state-level society (Kantor 1944; Arkell and Ucko 1965; Fattovich 1984).

By 3100 BC this state encompassed even Lower Egypt (Hassan 1985; Hoffman 1982; Wilson 1951). Here, during much of the fourth millennium BC, quite complex, ranked communities such as Ma'adi and Buto were involved in long distance trade with the ancient Near Eastern cultures (Kantor 1965; Rizkana and Seeher 1985; van den Brink 1988; Wenke 1989).

The effects of Egypt's meteoric rise were also felt in Nubia. In Lower Nubia the Classic A-Group culture replaced the Abkan. A-Group-like populations are also known from Kerma in Upper Nubia (Bonnet et al. 1988).

Remains of the A-Group are found along the Nile from Kubania to Melik en Nasir, ca. 100 km south of Wadi Halfa (Nordström 1972). Radiocarbon dates and diagnostic Egyptian artifacts date the Classic and Terminal A-Group occupations to ca. 3500–3000 BC. A-Group populations lived in small semi-permanent settlements in the most fertile stretches of the Nile Valley (Trigger 1965; Nordström 1972). Most of the sites are deflated, but some, such as the sites near Saras, have in situ materials (Mills and Nordström 1966).

The Terminal A-Group site AFH-1 (Afiah) had stone house foundations (H.S.Smith 1962), while Khor Daud and the A-Group-like settlement at Kerma contained storage pits (Nordström 1972; Bonnet et al. 1988). The existence of large A-Group cemeteries—several containing double burials—confirms the picture of a relatively sedentary population. There are, however, some small ephemeral A-Group satellite camps as well (Trigger 1965).

The location of the A-Group settlements, the finds of sickle blades and numerous grinders, as well as macrobotanical remains of wheat, barley, and leguminous plants (Lal 1967; Nordström 1972) suggest a population heavily involved in agriculture. Hunting, gathering, and fishing also continued to be common activities.

Piotrovsky (1967) has argued that the A-Group population was nomadic and fully pastoral. This hypothesis, however, based on poorly documented arguments concerning the site of Khor Daud, is not generally accepted (Nordström 1972; W.Y. Adams 1977). Indeed, there is no strong evidence for any pastoral production by the A-Group: the presence of cattle is inferred only from ox-hides and possibly the dung tempered pottery (Nordström 1972). Whether the A-Group had a pastoral economic sector thus remains an open question.

It has been suggested that they obtained their pastoral products from specialized herders in the hinterlands (Nordström 1972). The presence of Red Sea shells in A-Group sites may represent trade with such herders east of the Nile (Hofmann 1967). Khor Daud has also been interpreted as a bartering market for the exchange of Nubian and Egyptian products (Nordström 1972). Its location in one of the richest A-Group locales near the mouth of Wadi Allaqi—the gateway to the Eastern Desert—led Nordström to the conclusion that the key to the prosperity of the A-Group culture lay in its role as intermediary in the cattle trade between the Eastern Desert nomads and the agriculturalists of Upper Egypt (1972). Unfortunately, however, the existence of such a nomadic pastoralist population in the Eastern Desert cannot be substantiated either archaeologically or textually for this period.

Circumstantially, however, the case for hinterland nomads is supported. The A-Group traded heavily with Egypt (Nordström 1972). Records indicate that Egypt, during the First Dynasty, imported ebony and ivory from Nubia (Säve-Söderbergh 1941), in return for which the Nubians principally received beer and wine (i.e., agricultural by-products, transported in Egyptian necked jars), as well as copper, other metals, and stone vessels (Nordström 1972; Trigger 1976; W.Y. Adams 1977). The question from where the A-Group (and the Naqada III population) received its pastoral products, in view of the lack of significant evidence for large scale pastoral production in the settlement patterns and faunal remains of either, is most reasonably answered by the assumption of trade with specialized pastoralists outside the Upper Egyptian and Lower Nubian Nile Valley.

During this time, two distinct populations, one in the Dongola Reach (Marks and Ferring 1971) and the other in the Kiseiba Plateau of the Western Desert (Connor 1984), may have been predominantly pastoral. On the Kiseiba Plateau, Connor (1984) found a number of Late Neolithic localities, predominantly dating to the late fourth millennium BC, which probably were the seasonal camps of mobile pastoralists. The Late Neolithic occupations of these marginal lands far exceeded those of the Middle

Neolithic period (Connor 1984), and were considerably more dispersed and ephemeral (Banks 1984). It is difficult to say whether these ephemeral occupations represent those of true nomads or only the herding sector of a village based mixed economy population. So far, in any case, semi-permanent or permanent settlements materially related to these ephemeral sites have not been found either in the Kiseiba Plateau or in the Nile Valley (Connor 1984), but Banks (1984) notes some similarities to the ceramics of the earlier Abkan Industry. If the absence of semi-permanent base settlements is not merely a result of insufficient survey coverage, there is good reason to believe that the Kiseiba population formed elements of a truly nomadic society.

The other predominantly pastoral group is found to the south, in the Dongola Reach of the Upper Nubian Nile Valley. The ceramics of the Karat Group suggest a population contemporaneous with the A-Group (Marks and Ferring 1971). There are no faunal remains associated with the 25 Karat Group sites. However, on the basis of the small, low density sites, the small lightweight pottery of the Karat, the rarity of grinding stones, the associated features (large hearths situated so as to provide a smoke screen against insects), and site locations in only those areas where grazing was available, it has been suggested that the sites were occupied in the dry season by goat herders (Marks and Ferring 1971). Presumably, their seasonal migratory rounds took them south and west of the river during the wet season (ibid.).

As with the Kiseiba herders, it is not certain whether the Karat sites represent the herding sector of a mixed economy society, or the remains of actual nomads. There have been no surveys away from the Nile which could document the rest of the Karat Group's settlement pattern. It is instructive, however, that there is no indication of Karat Group semi-permanent base settlements in the Nile Valley. This situation, in contrast to all other earlier industries of the area, suggests that the Karat Group could afford to use the optimal Nile Valley only for pastoral purposes: a condition which surely argues against the presence of an intensively agricultural Karat sector in the southern and western hinterlands of the Dongola Reach. A predominantly pastoral adaptation, therefore, seems to be a reasonable assumption in the case of the Karat.

Overall, during Phase 3 most regions of northeast Africa experienced significant changes. The most remarkable was Egypt's transition to a state level society. The Lower Nubian A-Group expansion and increased specialization as an agricultural and trading society appears to have been partially a result of developments in Egypt. At roughly the same time that the populations of Upper Egypt and Lower Nubia were becoming more agriculturally oriented, other populations in the Western Desert and Upper Nubia seem to have become more pastorally oriented.

The developments which led to the appearance of nomadism in Upper Nubia and the Kiseiba Plateau during the last centuries of the third millennium BC fit closely to the pattern predicted by the symbiotic model (chapter 1). In the beginning there were only mixed economy populations at apparently low levels of political and social complexity (e.g., the Abkan and the Khartoum Neolithic). Along with the rise of a more complex society in Upper Egypt after 4000 BC, as indicated by large and rich Amratian tombs (Hoffman 1982), there are weak indications that the population turned to the more specialized agropastoral adaptation. By the time the state and intensive agriculture appeared in Upper Egypt, we find evidence for nomadic pastoral populations in the Upper Nubian and Kiseiba hinterlands, as well as possible evidence for trade between hinterland and heartland through the A-Group intermediaries. The symbiosis model's predicted trajectory to nomadism thus fits the archaeological sequence from Upper Egypt and Nubia between 4500 and 3000 BC.

Alternativly, a case can also be made for the role of ecological factors in nomadism among the Kiseiba population. The end of the Playa II formation in the Western Desert at about 3500 BC—a time of transition from grasslands to desert (Schild and Wendorf 1984)—corresponds more or less with the time the Kiseiba herders appeared on the scene. Banks (1984) is of the opinion that there is a causal correlation between these events.

The same, however, cannot be said about the Karat population. Inhabiting the Nile Valley itself, they were surely not forced into a predominantly pastoral adaptation by aridity; that Upper Nubian stretch of the Nile could, as it did 500 years later, support large, sedentary agricultural populations (the Kerma culture).

Other ecological factors like population pressure are hardly applicable either. To suggest that the Kiseiba population became nomadic after being pushed out of optimal zones by an increase in population requires some evidence for real over-population. Continued rise in the Upper Egyptian Nile Valley population in succeeding centuries (Trigger 1965), however, tends to disprove this. There is even less evidence for population pressure in the Dongola Reach of this period.

Likewise, the other alternative explanation for the development of no-madism—warfare—is inapplicable to the Karat and Kiseiba cases. Al-though there is reason to believe that serious conflict between the Egyptian state and her neighbors did occur, it did so at the end of this sequence (ca. 3000 BC) and not in time to have driven the Kiseiba and Karat populations into a nomadic lifestyle.

The magnitude of this conflict may be indicated by a hiatus in occupation of all archaeologically known stretches of the Nile Valley south of Egypt's ancient border after 3000 BC and until about 2500 BC. Shortly after power in Egypt became centralized at the beginning of the Early Dynastic Period, the A-Group occupation of Lower Nubia abruptly ended (W.Y. Adams 1977; Nordström 1972; Trigger 1976). For all intents and purposes, it ap-pears that the Lower Nubian Nile Valley was abandoned by the A-Group shortly after the transition from Naqada III to Early Dynastic times. The only archaeological remains of Lower Nubia dating between 3000 and 2500 BC are Old Kingdom Egyptian fortified towns (Nordström 1972; Trigger 1976; W.Y. Adams 1977), which lead to the speculation that conflict drove the A-Group population into the deserts bordering the Nile.

Upper Nubia may have been abandoned as well. In the Dongola Reach there are no known archaeological occurrences postdating the Karat Group. Elsewhere, in the Kerma area, the A-Group-like occupation is not securely dated, but it could conceivably fall into the period of Lower Nubia's occupational hiatus (Privati 1988).

The depopulation of the Nubian Nile Valley is most convincingly at-tributed to a change in Egypt's foreign policy concerning her relations with the south (Nordström 1972). Whereas in the previous phase the Nubians traded with Egypt, after the Second Dynasty Egypt seems to have taken outright control of that trade (W.Y. Adams 1977; Trigger 1976). The new attitude of Egypt toward its southern neighbors can best be seen in the relief at Jebel Sheikh Suleiman, which probably dates to the Early Dynastic Period (Arkell 1950), and in the victory stela of Khasekhem at Hierakon-polis (Säve-Söderbergh 1941), both of which speak of Egyptian attacks into Lower Nubia. It seems that that which Egypt was previously prepared to trade for, it was now willing to take by force.

The effects of such a shift in Egyptian policy must have had a cataclysmic impact on the Nubians. Repeated raids, perhaps like Senefru's during Fourth Dynasty—which according to the Palermo stone, bagged him some 200,000 head of cattle (Breasted 1906)—would have decimated the Nubians. Abandoning the Nile Valley (Egypt's principal route of penetration into Nubia) may have been the only option left.

Interestingly, the shock of Egypt's campaigns may even have rippled as far south as the Middle Nile region. There are no known archaeological remains in the Middle Nile Valley which postdate the Late Neolithic occupation at Kadada (ca. 3000 BC at the latest, Geus 1986). Not until the Meroitic times (first millennium BC) did populations return to that stretch of the Nile in any numbers. Even in the hinterlands of the Middle Nile, Shaqadud seems to have been abandoned until ca. 2600–2700 BC, when a late Neolithic occupation was resumed (Marks et al. 1985).

Conflict of this magnitude clearly disrupted existing economic relations between Egypt and her hinterlands through the intermediary of the A-Group. Now, if the displaced Lower Nubian A-Group turned to nomadism in the hinterlands, the conflict model could be supported. But there is yet no secure indication of the fate of the A-Group. In any event, it remains clear that nomadism—as perhaps represented by the Kiseiba and Karat Group herders—can arise in the absence of conflict with a state. Similar conclusions are suggested in the next chapter, which examines nomadism in the Nubian hinterlands between ca 2500 and 1100 BC.

Chapter VII
Nomads in the Eastern Desert

2500–1100 BC

The events described below touch on the developments in Nubia during the second half of the third and most of the second millennia BC (Fig. 7.1). An actual case of developing nomadism is not documented in this sequence: that development seems to have happened somewhat earlier. During this period—which for the purpose of description is divided into four segments (2500–2100 BC; 2100–1750 BC; 1750–1500 BC; and 1500–1100 BC)—the post-Neolithic arid phase was in effect (Muzzolini 1982). It is documented by lower lake levels and dune formation at Chad (Servant and Servant-Vildary 1980), deflation and dune formation in the Sahel (Talbot 1980), drying of the Mauritanian Lakes (Petit-Maire 1979), progressing dunes and minimal Wadi activity in Nubia and Egypt (Butzer 1975), and lower lake levels at Turkana and the Ethiopian lakes (Livingstone 1980; Gasse et al., 1980). In the eastern Sahara the savanna began to retreat in the early fourth millennium BC, and present arid conditions were attained by the second millennium BC (Neumann 1989).

2500–2100 BC (Fig. 7.2)

Perhaps partly because of the onset of drier conditions, the Nubian Nile Valley, which had been all but depopulated in 3000 BC, began once again to be inhabited. In Upper Nubia around 2600 BC the Kerma Ancien culture left substantial remains at Sai and Kerma (Gratien 1978; Bonnet et al. 1982). The Kerma Ancien ceramics bear some resemblance to those of the A-Group-like pre-Kerma assemblage (Privati 1988). They are also similar to some of the examples from the Kadada Late Neolithic in the Middle Nile region (Geus 1979).

At Sai Island the Kerma Ancien occupation is extremely large but has no depth of deposits, and it is possible that the inhabitants were seasonally quite mobile, as Gratien (1978) suggests. Some sixty Kerma Ancien burials at Sai (Gratien 1978; Vercoutter 1958), however, suggest a long period of occupation.

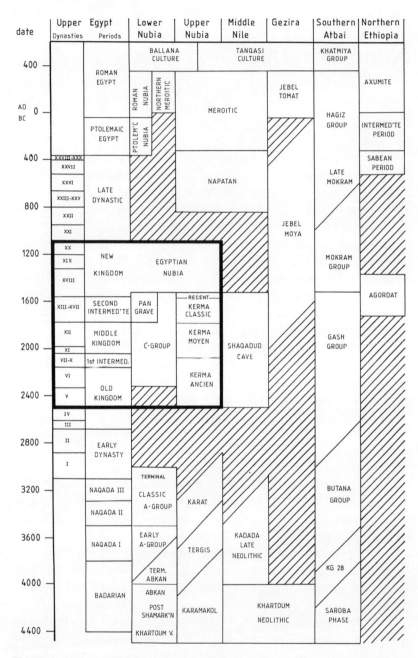

Figure 7.1. Egypt and Nubia, 2500–1100 BC.

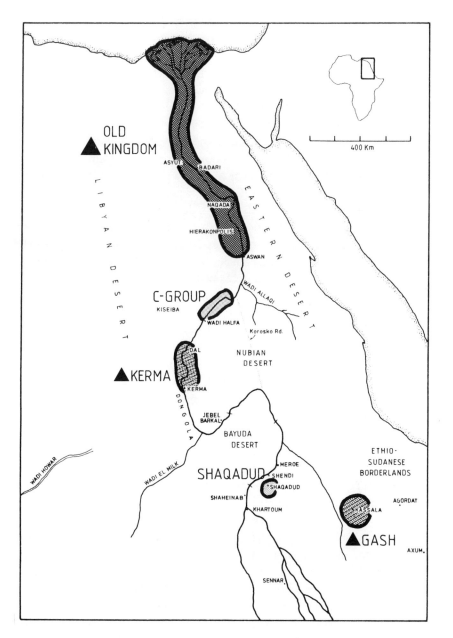

Figure 7.2. Northeast Africa, 2500–2100 BC. For key to symbols see figures in chapter 6.

At the site of Kerma, on the other hand, the population was apparently quite sedentary. The Kerma Ancien levels there show an impressive over-lapping of postholes (Bonnet et al. 1982). Grain bins and a defensive wall around the Ancien settlement at Kerma (Bonnet et al. 1984, 1986) add to the impression of a sedentary population. Sacrificed domestic animals and ox-hides found in the Ancien burials at Kerma (Bonnet et al. 1982) suggest pastoralism, but probably not at Kerma itself. Since Kerma was located along the Nile and included features indicating a sedentary agricultural population, intensive pastoral production at Kerma itself seems unlikely. It seems likelier that another segment of Kerma population, perhaps similar to the ones at Sai, or even other non-Kerma populations in the hinterlands supplied the sacrificial animals and their hides. Some Kerma Ancien graves, as at Kadruka, are notably poorer than the Ancien graves at the site of Kerma (Bonnet et al. 1986; Reinold 1987), suggesting perhaps some level of status differentiation in Kerma Ancien society, and also perhaps a "rural/ urban" division of the population. As with the Naqada I society of Egypt a thousand years before, there is too little data to confirm an agropastoral adaptation, but the clues are tantalizing.

About the same time or a little later, Lower Nubia was re-inhabited, this time by the early C-Group populations. Bietak's (1968) stage Ia of the C-Group is cross-dated, using Egyptian artifacts, to the early part of the First Intermediate Period (ca. 2100 BC), but Bonnet (et al. 1982) argues for an earlier date on the basis of ceramic similarities between Kerma Ancien and the early C-Group.

In any case, the early C-Group faunal remains from Sayala suggest an economy partially reliant on pastoralism (Bietak 1986). Furthermore, some stone walls at that site suggest a possible corral (ibid.). Considering the near absence of grinding implements at the Early C-Group sites, Bietak (1986) suggests that agriculture was not an important aspect of their subsis-tence strategy. Nevertheless, a nomadic pastoral adaptation was not the case either. The settlements of the early C-Group suggest a fairly sedentary population. At Aniba and Sayala (Bietak 1968, 1986), stage Ia C-Group habitations include several hut circles, with postholes reinforced with basal rocks, while at Aniba N there is a large early C-Group cemetery. A mixed economy appears a more reasonable interpretation of the evidence.

During this period there was considerable commerce between Egypt and her Nubian neighbors—the Kerma and C-Group population—much as there had been 500–1000 years earlier between Egypt and the Nubian

A-Group. The Sixth Dynasty princes of Elephantine mounted numerous expeditions to Nubia and even farther to Punt (Säve-Söderbergh 1941; Trigger 1965; Kitchen 1982), a part of which was perhaps the Southern Atbai of the middle Kassala Phase (Fattovich 1985). The biography of Harkhuf, inscribed at Kubbet-el-Hawa opposite Aswan, speaks of overland trade expeditions to the land of Yam (Sethe 1932), which may have referred to Kerma (Edel 1955, but see also O'Connor 1986). Significantly, the inscription speaks of a military escort provided by the sovereign of Yam assigned to protect the expedition on their way through the territories of other chieftains (Trigger 1965), among whom one might reasonably include the C-Group population.

Reisner's (1923) discovery of Sixth Dynasty stone vessels at Kerma provides the archaeological evidence for this trade. Texts suggest that both the Kerma and the C-Group cultures received honey, ointments, beer and wine, linen, copper, and luxury goods from Egypt, in return for which cattle, sheep, and goats, as well as ebony, ivory, incense, oils, and panther skins were exported by the Nubians (Sethe 1932; Säve-Söderbergh 1941; Bietak 1986). Kerma, most notably in later phases, was apparently the middleman in the overland trade link between Punt and Egypt, which began as early as the Sixth Dynasty, ca. 2300–2200 BC (Kitchen 1982; Fattovich 1985).

This wide-ranging commerce included domesticated animals and their secondary products. The agricultural Egyptians, mixed economy early C-Group, and possibly agropastoral Kerma Ancien populations, however, do not seem to have been intensively engaged in pastoral production. Whether pastoral segments of the Kerma population, or nomads in the hinterlands supplied the pastoral goods remains unknown for this period.

2100–1750 BC (Fig. 7.3)

By 2000 BC, however, one can infer the presence of nomads in the Eastern Desert from Egyptian texts of the Twelfth Dynasty (the Semna Despatches, Smither 1945) which make several references to the Medjay desert dwellers living east of the Nile. Principally these military reports speak of denying to Medjay escaping the drought in the hinterlands access to the Nile Valley. Most researchers assume (considering the aridity of the Eastern Desert) that the Medjay were probably a pastoral nomadic popula-

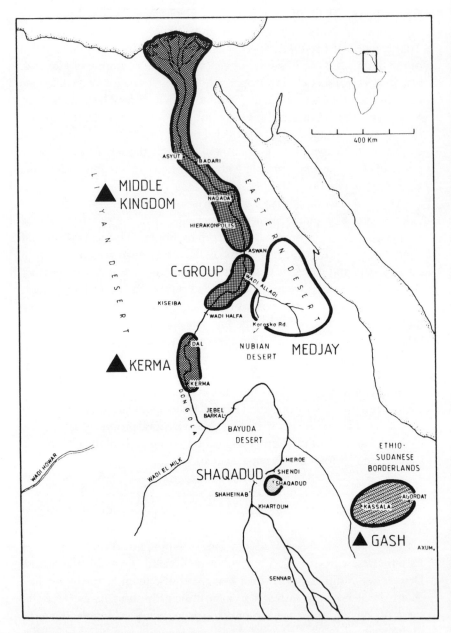

Figure 7.3. Northeast Africa, 2100–1750 BC. For key to symbols see figures in chapter 6.

tion, although this assumption remains untested. The suggestion is to some extent supported by the tomb drawings from Meir (Blackman 1914, 1915a, 1915b), dating to the Twelfth Dynasty, which show Egyptian cattle in the care of Medjay herders.

By 2000 BC, Egypt, having regained its political stability in the Middle Kingdom Period after an episode of political breakdown during the First Intermediate Period (ca. 2181–2133/2040 BC), embarked on a new round of vigorous commerce with the cultures to the south (Steindorff 1937; Reisner 1923; Säve Söderbergh 1941). During the Middle Kingdom Period (2133/2040–1786 BC), Egypt protected her trade interests in Nubia with a string of mighty forts built along the Nile (Emery 1965; Säve-Söderbergh 1941). The main source of commerce in Nubia was Kerma, which, by now, during its Moyen period, had grown to a sizeable mudbrick town with a strong politico-religious leadership which manifested itself in elaborate burials and the monumental structures of the Deffufas (Reisner 1923; Bonnet et al. 1982, 1984, 1986; Gratien 1978).

At this time in Lower Nubia, the C-Group population lived to a great extent under the control of Egypt and its military forts like the ones at Aniba and Buhen. The Lower Nubian copper and diorite mines continued to be exploited by Egypt (Weigall 1907; Säve-Söderbergh 1941). Trade between Egypt and the C-Group had dropped off (Bietak 1968). In the absence of settlement hierarchies, and with only weak status differentiation in the C-Group graves of this time, however, their social and political organization appears to have remained at a relatively simple level (Trigger 1976).

The C-Group population of this time lived a settled life in small villages along the Nile River. At sites such as Aniba, single room circular structures and multi-room curvilinear ones have been excavated (Steindorff 1937). C-Group sites during this phase were located in the most fertile stretches of the valley, but areas which required irrigation for agriculture were left uninhabited (Trigger 1965).

The settlement patterns of the C-Group and Kerma populations of this time bespeak a sedentary agricultural adaptation. However, because of the preponderance of cattle art, livestock sacrifices, and ox-hides in their burials, they are often assumed to have been predominantly pastoralist (Emery 1965; Arkell 1961). It is more likely that, as W.Y. Adams (1977) put it, they aspired to be cattle owners. As their settlements suggest, the valley dwellers themselves were certainly not intensively engaged in pastoral production.

With additional work, it may come to light that the C-Group and Kerma cultures had pastoral sections inhabiting the immediate hinterlands of the Nile, but it seems more likely that the independent Medjay were the principal suppliers of pastoral products in circulation at this time. Other suppliers may have been further south. In the Middle Nile region, tumulus 3 at Jebel Makbor may belong to a pastoralist of this period (Lenoble 1987).

In this light, the Kerma population may have fulfilled a role similar to the one suggested for the A-Group of a millennium earlier, playing the role of the middleman in the commerce between Egypt and her hinterland no-mads, a role it may have also played between Egypt and the eastern Sudan (Fattovich 1985; Fattovich et al., 1988).

1750–1500 BC (Fig. 7.4)

After 1750 BC, relations between the Egyptian state and the Medjay changed. During Egypt's Second Intermediate Period—a time of turmoil and internal divisions brought about by the Hyksos invasion of Lower Egypt (Wilson 1951; W.Y.Adams 1977)—the princes of Upper Egypt, in their bid to defeat the Hyksos, went so far as to recruit Medjay as mercen-aries (Säve-Söderbergh 1941; Bietak 1966).

The Pan-Graves found in Lower Nubia and Upper Egypt apparently belong to these Medjay mercenaries (Bietak 1966, 1986; Säve-Söderbergh 1941). Most of the Pan-Graves are found in the C-Group's stretch of the Nile, but anthropometric analyses show that the two populations were quite distinct (Ehgartner and Jungwirth 1966; Bietak 1986). Despite the graves, the Medjay do not seem to have actually lived in the Nile Valley. Aside from their one known camp-spot near Khor Wadi Nashriya (Bietak 1966), there are no actual habitation sites with Pan-Grave type artifacts found in the Nile Valley. It seems that the Medjay, for the most part, continued to live in the desert.

In Nubia the weakening of Egypt's power coincided with the flowering of the Nubian cultures. Kerma in its Classic period filled the political and commercial vacuum left by Egypt. Massive burial tumuli of the Kerma nobles accompanied by a host of sacrificial victims, the monumental archi-tecture and irrigation schemes at Kerma, as well as the occupation of the erstwhile Egyptian forts in Lower Nubia by the Kerma culture attest to the wide power and influence of the Kerma Classic state society (Säve-Söder-bergh 1941; Bonnet et al. 1982–1986; Gratien 1978).

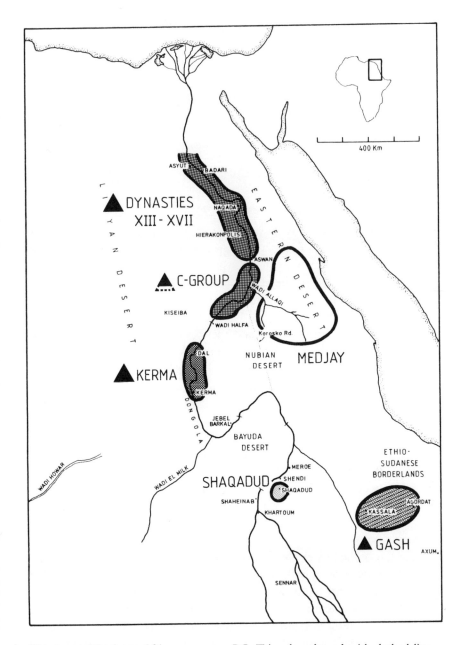

Figure 7.4. Northeast Africa, 1750–1500 BC. Triangle enlarged with dashed line represents possible state level organization. For explanation of other symbols see figures in chapter 6.

The C-Group population of Lower Nubia, probably allied with Kerma, also went through its classic period during this phase (Bietak 1968). This is shown by the occupation of large mudbrick towns, some of which, like Areika, Karanog, and Wadi es Sebua, had fortification walls and castles (MacIver and Woolley 1909; Sauneron 1965). The stately burials of the C-Group princes of this period attest to the richness and complexity of the society (Steindorff 1937).

1500–1100 BC (Fig. 7.5)

This prosperity did not outlive Egypt's Second Intermediate Period. The New Kingdom Period (1500–1100 BC) can be characterized by Egypt's outright colonization of Nubia (W.Y.Adams 1977). Unlike the situation in the Old Kingdom Period, when Egypt's heavy handed foreign policy of direct acquisition led to the abandonment of the entire Nile Valley, the Egyptian policy during the New Kingdom Period resulted in the acculturation of the Nubians.

Gone were the Kerma kings and their extensive trade network. With Egyptian occupation of Nubia as far south as the Fourth Cataract (Sethe 1906), occupation at Kerma ceased and the Deffufas were burnt down (Gratien 1978). Nubians, now under the administration of the Viceroy of Kush, became gradually Egyptianized.

The Egyptianization of Upper Nubia began in the Kerma Recent Phase (Gratien 1978) with the building of an Egyptian military fort at the north end of Dongola (Emery 1965). Both Tuthmose I and II sacked Nubia, and later pharaohs appropriated harvest, cattle, slaves, gold, ebony, and ivory—the traditional exports of Nubia—as tribute (Sethe 1906). The acculturation of the Upper Nubian population is documented in burials which are indistinguishable from those of ordinary Egyptians (Trigger 1976; W.Y. Adams 1977).

The fate of the Lower Nubians was similar. The stage III of the C-Group culture, contemporary with the Kerma Recent Phase, witnessed the gradual acculturation of the Nubians into Egyptian culture (Bietak 1968). C-Group burials became identical to the ordinary Egyptian ones, and the once independent culture essentially vanished (Emery 1965; W.Y.Adams 1977). Egyptian staff and administrators occupied the main population centers of Lower Nubia (Trigger 1965). Nubian nobles were taken and schooled in

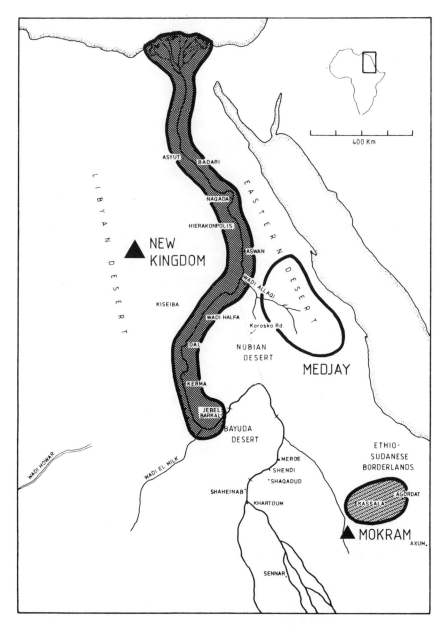

Figure 7.5. Northeast Africa, 1500–1100 BC. For key to symbols see figures in chapter 6.

Egyptian ways to provide a local ruling elite with strong loyalties to Egypt (W.Y. Adams 1977). Egyptian garrisons reoccupied the Lower Nubian forts which had fallen into the hands of the Kerma culture during the Second Intermediate Period, and Egypt again began the process of mining for gold and other precious commodities in the region (Säve-Söderbergh 1941).

The agricultural Nubians had become much like the felaheen of Egypt proper (Emery 1965; W.Y. Adams 1977). And, indeed, population levels in Nubia soared at this time, as the region was added to Egyptian territory (Trigger 1965). The Amon Temple built at Jebel Barkal near the Fourth Cataract (Reisner 1917) provides a cogent symbol of the completeness of Egypt's ideological and political takeover of Nubia.

The takeover affected even the Medjay. Their mercenaries became Egyptianized, as indicated by the continued use of the term "Medjay" to denote a corps of the Egyptian army, in spite of the disappearance of Pan-Graves from the archaeological record (Bietak 1966). The Medjay of the hinterlands proper, in turn, must have been affected by Egypt's large scale gold-mining operations in the Eastern Desert (Säve-Söderbergh 1941). It seems likely that they would have provided Egypt with a ready source of man-power for the backbreaking task of extracting gold. The New Kingdom texts of Amenhotep IV and Tuthmose IV seem to refer to raids against the Medjay (DeMorgan et al. 1894; MacIver and Woolley 1911; Säve-Söderbergh 1941). Under such circumstances, it is likely that the Medjay scattered to the four winds, probably seeking refuge in the Red Sea hills much as the modern Beja do in times of trouble.

Some elements of the Medjay seem to have gone far to the south. In the Southern Atbai around 1500 BC, there began the late Kassala Phase occupation which differed from the previous middle Kassala Phase occupation mainly insofar as its associated material culture was identical to that of the Pan-Grave cultures, that is, to that of the archaeologically known Medjay mercenaries of the Second Intermediate Period (Sadr 1987). Although there is no evidence that the Medjay themselves occupied the Kassala area of the Southern Atbai, the changes in the ceramic styles suggest that the native population of the Southern Atbai culturally became Medjay (Sadr 1990): an event which takes on added significance considering the possibility suggested by Fattovich (1985) that the Kassala area was a part of Punt at that time. The presence of Pan-Grave-like artifacts on some of the Agordat sites (Arkell 1954) suggests that a similar situation applied to parts of northern Ethiopia, as well.

Overall, the Medjay nomads played a major role in the events of the period, but they remain known only from the fringes of their culture area. Whether they were in fact nomadic throughout this period remains unknown in the absence of direct archaeological data from the Eastern Desert. Assuming, however, as the bulk of the data suggest, that they were indeed nomadic, what can be said about their origins? Direct data are unavailable, but three hypothetical possibilities can be put forward.

The first hypothesis is that they were originally a Nile Valley population displaced to the desert: a condition which would favor the ecological interpretation of nomadism (chapter 1). Egyptian texts of the Sixth Dynasty (ca. 2400–2200 BC) refer to an area in the Lower Nubian Nile Valley as the Land of Mdj (Sethe 1932), suggesting that the Medjay of later years may have originally inhabited the Lower Nubian Nile along with, or as part of the early C-Group. Such a scenario suggests population pressure in the valley, displacement of a segment to the hinterlands, and consequent nomadism in the absence of other viable subsistence strategies.

Second, it is plausible that the Medjay had been in the Eastern Desert since Naqada III times, about a thousand years earlier. There is some evidence for nomads from that period (chapter 6), in which case the question of their origins has already been discussed.

The third scenario seems more tenable, and it can account for the origins of the C-Group and Kerma cultures which appeared on the scene during this period, as well. The Medjay (Pan-Grave), C-Group, and Kerma remains, especially their ceramics, grave superstructures, and the burials themselves, differ significantly from each other, indicating that all three were independent cultural entities (Gratien 1978). There are, however, certain shared general similarities (such as a particular ceramic firing method which blackened the rims and interiors of the vessels) which perhaps suggest a common origin, possibly from the A-Group culture which disappeared from the Nile Valley around 3000 BC (chapter 6). A possible interpretation is that all three developed separately from splintered elements of the refugee A-Group population in the hinterlands of the Nile. One might propose that by ca. 2500 BC, with worsening climate in the hinterlands and perhaps a cessation of Egyptian hostilities (certainly by the First Intermediate Period), some of the now independent cultural descendants of the A-Group may have returned to the Nubian Nile Valley as the C-Group and Kerma cultures, while the Medjay stayed behind to pursue a nomadic pastoral way of life.

Such a scenario includes elements which could support any one of the rival hypotheses for the development of nomadism: warfare, ecological considerations, and also the symbiotic model. Without direct archaeological information from the Nubian hinterlands there is little point in supporting one of the hypotheses against the others.

Nevertheless, nomadism in the Eastern Desert of this period shows two facets which fit the symbiosis general model. The Medjay were active on the borders of a state-level agricultural society, and there is evidence for symbiotic relations between the two (as in the Twelfth Dynasty tomb paintings of Meir showing Medjay herders employed by Egyptians, and in the use of Medjay mercenaries by the Second Intermediate Period pharaohs of Upper Egypt).

In the next chapter, a closer fit is presented between the symbiosis model and nomadism in northeast Africa from the central and eastern Sudan of the first millennium BC.

Chapter VIII

Nomads on the Fringes of the Kushitic and Northern Ethiopian Kingdoms

Central Sudan 750 BC–AD 350

From 750 BC to AD 350 a number of nomadic societies are recorded on the fringes of the Upper Nubian and Middle Nile Valley Kushitic kingdom and the pre-Axumite and Axumite kingdoms of Northern Ethiopia (Fig. 8.1). Among these were the Hagiz Group nomads of the Southern Atbai, described in chapter 4.

Before the reign of the Kushitic kings of the Twenty-fifth Dynasty, which began around 750 BC, Nubia had lain practically uninhabited for some three centuries (W.Y. Adams 1977; Trigger 1976). The internal turmoil in Egypt from 1100 BC to ca. 750 BC, during which kings of Lybian, Nubian, Assyrian, and Persian origin ruled or sacked Lower Egypt (Wilson 1951), had brought down the vast trading network of Northeast Africa. It apparently also brought occupation in Nubia to an end.

Firth (1927) and W.Y. Adams (1977) argue that the depopulation of Nubia was caused by a lowering of the Nile, which made agriculture impossible in the steep-sided Nubian Nile Valley. Trigger (1976), however, disagrees, suggesting instead that political turmoil in Egypt and the cessation of gold production caused the abandonment. Whichever was the case, some of the Nubians (by then fully Egyptianized, see chapter 7) may have moved north to Egypt proper. Others may have joined the nomads in the desert. There is no evidence, however, to indicate that they moved south along the Nile. The Middle Nile region remained depopulated as it had been since late Neolithic times. Only the Amon Temple at Jebel Barkal seems to have remained inhabited and functioning during this extended interval from 1100 to 800 BC (Arkell 1961; Emery 1965).

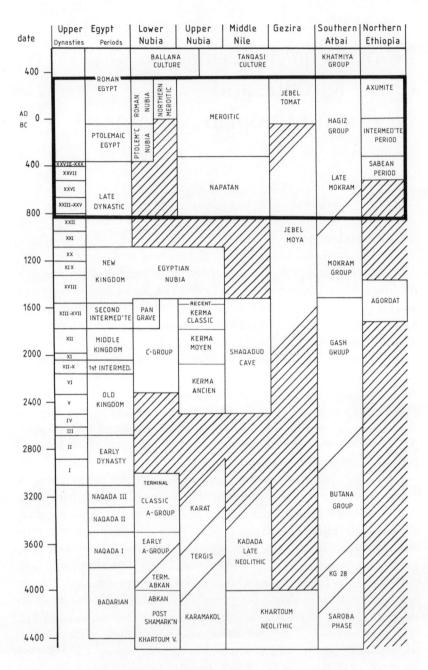

Figure 8.1. Central Sudan and northern Ethiopia, 750 BC–AD 350.

Sudan 750–350 BC (Fig. 8.2)

From Jebel Barkal arose the Kushitic Twenty-fifth Dynasty which briefly reunited Upper and Lower Egypt around 750 BC (Shinnie 1967). But barely a century later it fell to the onslaught of the Assyrian invasion, which once again divided Egypt (W.Y. Adams 1977; Trigger 1976). The Kushites, however, continued to rule over much of northern and central Sudan for nearly a millennium longer, first from their capital at Napata near Jebel Barkal, and later from Meroe on the Middle Nile.

The rise of this Kushitic dynasty out of a largely depopulated Upper Nubia is not yet fully understood. W.Y. Adams (1977) is of the opinion that an alliance betwen local hinterland chiefs and the priesthood at the Amon Temple of Jebel Barkal gave rise to the Napatan polity, the Kushitic dynasty, and eventually the Kushitic kingdom of northern and central Sudan. Some tumulus graves at Kurru, the earliest of which have been dated to ca. 850 BC (Reisner 1918; Trigger 1976), may represent the earliest reoccupation of Upper Nubia, perhaps by the hinterland populations. These graves contained quite a rich collection of goods and presumably belonged to the elite of society. Unfortunately, little is known about Napatan settlements.

The town of Meroe on the Middle Nile is better known (Shinnie 1967). The eighth century BC levels at Meroe contained mud brick houses as well as posthole circles of huts, large grain bins, abundant domesticated cattle, goat and sheep, as well as fish remains (Bradley 1984). A sedentary population with a mix of subsistence strategies seems to be indicated for this early Meroitic population.

Where these Meroites came from, like the question of the origins of the Napatans, remains enigmatic. The Middle Nile Valley itself had not seen significant occupation since the times of the Kadada late Neolithic (Geus 1986). Haaland (1981) is of the opinion that archaeologially invisible nomads occupied the region before Meroitic times. The only possible direct evidence for this comes from tumuli near Meroe, which are cross-dated to ca. 2000 BC and appear to belong to a pastoral population (Lenoble 1987; Privati 1987). At Shaqadud, 50 km east of the Middle Nile, there is evidence of occupation by a small mixed economy population ca. 2500 to 1500 BC (Marks et al. 1985). Interestingly, the Shaqadud cave overlooks a partly natural, partly man-made water pool, and the site is surrounded by a ring of ephemeral settlements which appear to represent remains of populations, perhaps pastoralists, relying on the Shaqadud water supply. The arrange-

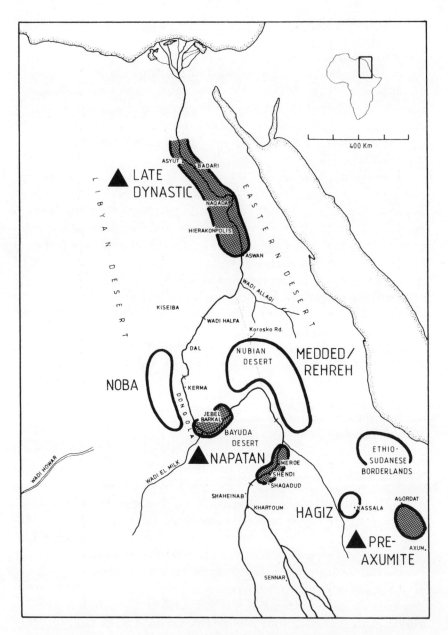

Figure 8.2. Northeast Africa, 750–350 BC. For key to symbols see figures in chapter 6 and 7.

ment seems vaguely prototypical of the Meroitic temple/hafir (man-made water catchment) complexes of some two millennia later.

Only at Jebel Moya, along the Nile south of Khartoum, may there have been a substantial settlement which spanned the Neolithic to Meroitic hiatus (Addison 1949). Napatan-Meroitic artifacts were found in some of the Jebel Moya graves, while Clark and Stemler (1975) acquired radiocarbon dates of 2250 ± 80 BC from another part of the site. If the site was occupied in the entire time spanning these two dates, it would be the only major population center on the Middle Nile preceding the Meroitic. But in fact so little else is known of Jebel Moya that it does not help to clear the enigma of the Meroites' origins.

Questions of origins aside, from the fact that the main Napatan sites are all located at the termini of major overland and riverine trade routes, as well as the presence of large amounts of imported wares, it is clear that trade played a major role in the functioning of the Kushite state (W.Y. Adams 1977). Its main export to Egypt was gold from the Eastern Desert mines, which had meanwhile fallen into Napatan hands (W.Y. Adams 1977). Since iron production had already begun in the early levels of occupation at Meroe (Bradley 1984), its export to southern lands may have formed part of the economy of Kush.

There are indications that the Kushitic state during its Napatan period was flanked to the east and west by nomads. Mention has already been made of the possibility that an alliance between hinterland nomads and the priesthood at Jebel Barkal gave rise to the Kushitic Dynasty. During the ascendancy of that dynasty and the reunification of Egypt these nomads may have composed the Napatan army. At times they may have been active on the trade routes to and from Egypt which ran overland on the Korosko road (W.Y. Adams 1977). At other times, texts show that the nomads were attacked by Napatans. The Kushite King Anlamani fought against the nomads, and so did a series of later kings who boasted of defeating the Rehreh and the Medded (probably Medjay) populations on the east side of the Nile Valley north of Meroe (Shinnie 1967).

Sudan 350 BC–AD 350 (Fig. 8.3)

After 350 BC, following Alexander's conquests, Egypt was reunified under the Ptolemaic Dynasties (Wilson 1951; Lloyd 1983), an event which

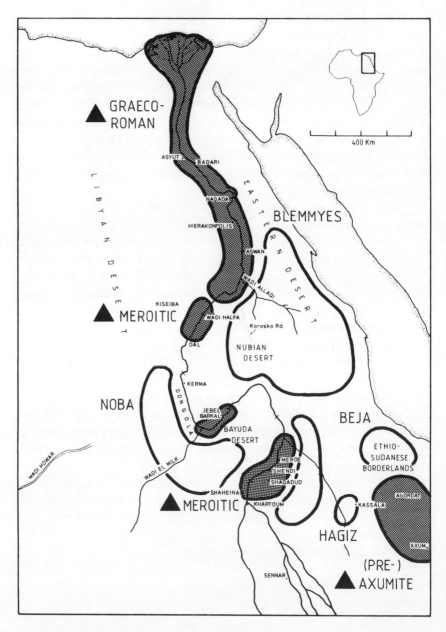

Figure 8.3. Northeast Africa, 350 BC–AD 350. For key to symbols see figures in chapter 6 and 7.

more or less coincided with the shift of the Kushitic kingdom's capital from Napata to Meroe (W.Y. Adams 1977; Shinnie 1967). Relations between Meroe and Ptolemaic Egypt were close, with Meroe importing luxury goods and exporting war elephants (Estigarribia 1982; Kobishchanov 1979). The Meroites by now were townspeople supported by an agricultural and perhaps mixed economy base population who farmed millet in the Nile Valley and the wadis leading to the river (Strabo *Geography* 17, 1,2 in W.Y. Adams 1977; Shinnie 1967).

After the death of Cleopatra in 30 BC, Egypt fell into the hands of the Roman Empire. The Meroitic kingdom, however, continued to dominate the Middle Nile. There were strong ties between Meroe and Roman Egypt, manifested in many Roman artifacts and architectural examples found among the ruins of the Meroitic towns (Kirwan 1978).

Indeed, Meroe may have been a client state of Rome at this time (W.Y. Adams 1977; Bradley 1984). A northern Meroitic population appeared in the southern half of Lower Nubia, a land which had lain abandoned since the Egyptian colony disappeared around 1100 BC (Trigger 1965).[1] The population which moved into Lower Nubia was culturally Meroitic, but without any of the palace or temple complexes associated with that culture's heartland in the Middle Nile region (W.Y. Adams 1977). The northern Meroitic people living in congested towns and villages such as Wadi el Arab (Emery and Kirwan 1935) and Arminna (Trigger 1967) were intensively occupied in agriculture and may have fed Roman Dodekaschoenos (northern Lower Nubia), an area with less than optimal agricultural potential (Griffith 1924). They also supplied Rome with the gold of Nubia (Kirwan 1982).

Apparently, throughout the Meroitic period nomads wandered in the grasslands of the Butana, playing the role of Meroe's (to use Toynbee's appropriate label) external proletariat (Bradley 1986; Strabo and Pliny in W.Y. Adams 1977). In the last few centuries BC the temple/hafir complexes (such as Musawwerat es Sufra and Naga) were constructed at the margin of the Butana pasturelands, which Bradley (1986) and others (Ali 1972; Arkell 1961) consider to have been the contact points between the sedentary agricultural Meroitic kingdom and the pastoral nomads of the Butana. The Butana Expedition of 1958 found only a large number of tumuli, rock drawings, and hafirs in the eastern Butana; they gained the impression that it was a region of stone age hunters and nomads (Hintze 1959).

More concrete evidence for the presence of nomads comes from some burials excavated at Geili (Caneva 1984, 1985a, 1988). The scattered graves contained pots dateable to roughly the third century BC. The pots resemble bottles used by modern nomads for transporting liquids, suggesting that the inhumations were of a nomadic population. Supporting evidence for the population's nomadism came from low strontium levels in their bones, a condition which was interpreted to show high reliance on a meat or, more likely, milk and blood diet (Coppa and Palmieri 1988). In addition, the isolated, dispersed graves and the absence of any settlements with related pottery led the excavator to the conclusion that a nomadic population was represented (Caneva 1988). The burial custom of this population, as defined by the shape of the grave, orientation of the body, and associated grave goods, differs from that indicated by typical graves at the site of Meroe (Shinnie 1967). Thus, it is assumed that they represent members of a culturally independent nomadic regional population.

Classical texts indicate that the entire eastern flank of the Meroitic kingdom was inhabited by the Beja nomadic groups (probably descendants of the Medjay, see chapter 7), while the western flank was occupied by Noba nomads (W.Y. Adams 1979). Both these populations may have been involved in the Meroitic overland trade traffic. The acquisition of camels in the last few centuries BC must have made the nomads particularly adept at alternating their role from caravaniers to raiders (Trigger 1965). Indeed, Eratosthenes (third century BC), and Strabo (end of first century BC) described the Noba of the Bayuda as nomadic brigands threatening the Meroitic trade routes (Strabo *Geography* 17, 1, 2 in W.Y. Adams 1977; Kirwan 1974, 1972b).

Northern Ethiopia and Eastern Sudan 750 BC–AD 350

750/500–350 BC (Fig. 8.2)

Nomads were also active in this period far to the east on the borders of the northern Ethiopian kingdoms. Around the fifth century BC, or somewhat earlier, a pre-Axumite culture appeared in highland Ethiopia (Fattovich 1984d; Anfray 1968). This period of Ethiopian ancient history, known as the Ethiopian-Sabean Period (Fattovich 1984d), witnessed the appearance of a politically and economically complex society in northern

Ethiopia, the iconography of which showed many similarities to contemporaneous South Arabian cultures. Since so little is known about the preceding cultures of the area, it is not clear how much of the impetus for the development of the pre-Axumite kingdom came from indigenous groups and how much was introduced from Arabia.

Coincident with the rise of complex state societies in the Middle Nile region, and somewhat later in northern Ethiopia, there was a major disjunction in the Southern Atbai, as described in chapter 4. Whereas until ca. 1100 BC Egypt, Kerma, and Punt (Southern Atbai?) had formed the major axis of interaction in Northeast Africa, after 750 BC the axis shifted to include Egypt, Kush, and the kingdoms of northern Ethiopia. The Southern Atbai had become a politically and economically (not ecologically) marginal zone, and became occupied by the Hagiz nomads of the Taka Phase.

350 BC– AD 1 (Fig. 8.3)

Around 350 BC, the pre-Axumite culture during its intermediate period lost many of its South Arabian traits and became recognizably more Ethiopian (Anfray 1967). The sites of the pre-Axumites suggest a sedentary agricultural population with masonry towns complete with temples and other monumental art and architecture, such as Hawlti and Melazo (Leclant 1959; Anfray 1965; Fattovich 1984d), villages such as Ona Hachel (Anfray 1970), and towns such as Matara and Yeha (Fattovich 1972; Anfray and Annequin 1965). The base population practiced plough agriculture (Fattovich 1984d). The port of Adulis, the main Northeast African gateway for trade to areas as far away as India and Ceylon, began operation during the intermediate period (Anfray 1967).

The trade routes from highland Ethiopia to the Nile, which would have run down the length of the Atbara (Kobishchanov 1979), could have provided the Hagiz Group nomads with profitable opportunities. Contact between the Southern Atbai and northern Ethiopia is attested by the presence of some pre-Axumite sherds found in the Hagiz Group sites (Fattovich, Marks, and Mohammed-Ali 1984). Perhaps the Hagiz Group can be equated with the Megabaroi nomadic herders occupying the Gash Delta region, who are known to us through the accounts of the classical geographer Agatharchides (in Fattovich 1987).

AD 1–350 (Fig. 8.3)

By the beginning of the Christian era, the Axumite kingdom reigned over northern Ethiopia (Kobishchanov 1979). The Beja nomads of the northern Ethio-Sudanese borderlands were economically connected with or even dependent on the Axumite state. Pastoral production played a large role in this interdependency: King Ezana II is recorded to have given some twenty-five thousand head of cattle to a Beja group (Kobishchanov 1979). Possibly, as their Medjay ancestors did for the Twelfth Dynasty Egyptians (see chapter 7), the Beja nomads looked after the Axumites' herds. Bordering the Axumite kingdom, the Hagiz nomads of the Southern Atbai may have been similarly associated with the highland state.

Their association, however, does not seem to have lasted long. Sometime between AD 325 and 350 the Axumite King Ezana II campaigned against Meroe. This much is known from his inscriptions left behind at Meroe and Axum (Kobishchanov 1979). On his way to Meroe, Ezana stopped to defeat the local nomads—perhaps including the Hagiz Group—at Kemalke ford, located a few miles upstream from Khashm el Girba on the Atbara River (Hintze 1967). Having defeated them, Ezana packed them off (six tribes comprising four thousand souls, Kirwan 1974) to another part of his kingdom, and continued across the Butana steppe to the Gezira (Kirwan 1972b). Meroitic towns in that area and in the north, at the confluence of the Atbara and the Nile, had apparently fallen into the hands of the Noba, who, it will be remembered, previously operated as nomads in the desert west of the Nile (Kirwan 1972b). Meroe itself was still functioning, so Ezana sacked it and erected his victory stela there. The combination of Ezana's attack, changes in Rome's frontier policy (see next chapter), and the ascendancy of the rival trading kingdom at Axum, all appear to have conspired to bring about the end of the Meroitic kingdom's hegemony in the Sudan (W.Y. Adams 1977; Kirwan 1972a,b).

The depopulation of the Southern Atbai after the Taka Phase was possibly a result of Ezana's campaigns, which ultimately took him to Meroe. Perhaps the Southern Atbai became a no-man's land, a buffer zone between the Axumite kingdom and the Noba occupiers of the Middle Nile region. In any event, other hinterlanders in the northern Ethio-Sudanese borderlands—exhaustively listed in such documents as the Adulis and Ezana's inscriptions (Kirwan 1972a,b; Kobishchanov 1979), and in the accounts of classical geographers such as Agatharchides and Eratosthenes (Kirwan

1972b; Fattovich 1987)—continued their economic links with the Axumite kingdom (Kobischchanov 1979).

Thus, overall, in the Sudan and Ethiopia of the first millennia BC and AD, symbiosis seems to have been the principal aspect of nomad/sedentary relations. The information, for example, suggests that nomad caravaniers operated on the flanks of the Meroitic kingdom and perhaps on the Atbara route between Axum and Meroe. Ezana's gift herds to the Beja of the northern Ethio-Sudanese borderlands may also show the existence of such symbiotic links.

This evidence tends to negate the significance of conflict in shaping nomadism. Indeed, the major episode of conflict in this period, Ezana's campaign, may have spelt the end of nomadism in the Southern Atbai. Events in the north from roughly the same time, which are described in the next chapter, also indicate that conflict was not a decisive factor in the development and maintenance of northeast African nomadism.

Chapter IX

Nomads on the Southern Border of Roman Egypt

Nubia ca. AD 1–500

The nomads of Nubia during Ptolemaic and Roman times are known purely from textual references. Nevertheless, combined with the known archaeological sequence (Fig. 9.1), the available information supports the symbiosis view of nomadism better than the conflict model.

From the preceding period, there are many classical references to nomads who inhabited the Nubian hinterlands in Ptolemaic times (e.g., Herodotus, iv. 183; Artemiodorus, quoted in Diodorus, iii, 32–33). While the Ptolemies inhabited the northern half of Lower Nubia (the Dodekaschoenos) and controlled the gold mines of the Eastern Desert, Agatharchides (130 BC) describes how the depopulated southern half of Lower Nubia was occasionally visisted by desert nomads to water their herds (Trigger 1965; Murray 1967).

After 30 BC, the Dodekaschoenos became heavily fortified by a string of Roman military stations, presumably to ward off the nomads of the Eastern Desert (Demicheli 1976). Shortly thereafter, southern Lower Nubia was inhabited by a northern Meroitic population, who also supplied Roman Egypt with the gold of Nubia (Kirwan 1982).

In AD 289—not long before Meroe finally fell to the Axumites—Rome abandoned the Dodekaschoenos (Fig. 9.2), perhaps as a result of the incessant raids by these nomads (Trigger 1965), or perhaps because of changes in her frontier zone policies (Kirwan 1974, 1978). With Rome's retreat, the gold and emerald mines of the Eastern Desert fell into the hands of the Blemmye Beja nomads, and trade in emeralds to Axum became an important part of their economy (Kobishchanov 1979). It will be remembered from the last chapter that the Beja in the south, bordering the Eritrean highlands, were around this time receiving gifts of 25,000 head of cattle from Ezana (Kobishchanov 1979).

By the time Meroe was defeated by Ezana (chapter 8), she had already lost some of her settlements in the Nile/Atbara confluence to the Noba

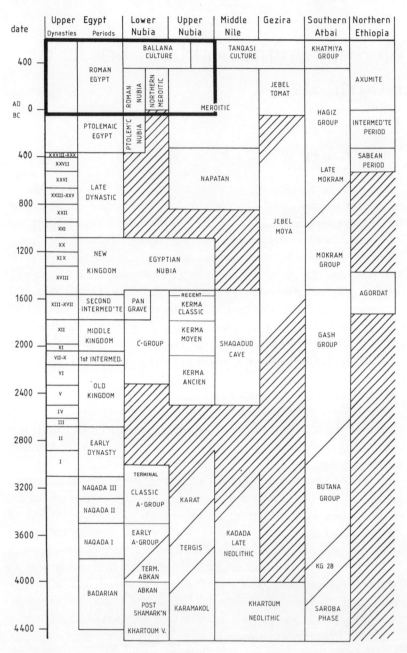

Figure 9.1. Nubia, AD 1–500.

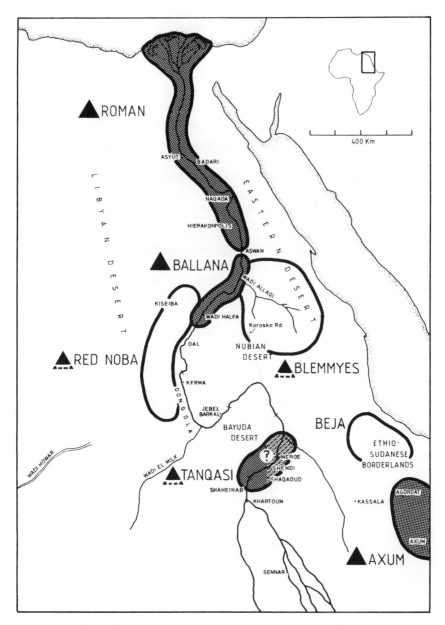

Figure 9.2. Northeast Africa, ca. AD 300–500. For key to symbols see figures in chapter 6 and 7.

nomads (Kirwan 1972b). With the complete fall of Meroe, the Noba (n.b., Ezana refers to these as the Black Noba, Kobischchanov 1979) seem to have occupied the entire Middle Nile from Dongola to Sennar in the Gezira (Trigger 1965; Kirwan 1982). These Noba, archaeologically manifested as the Tanqasi culture, lived in the ill-repaired Meroitic towns and also in villages of reed huts (Kirwan 1982). Ezana's records indicate that they were cultivators. The archaeological record indicates that the post-Meroitic population was indigenous—culturally changed but not replaced by outsiders (Lenoble 1987a).

Other Noba (Ezana's Red Noba) took over southern Lower, and Upper Nubia from Dongola to the Dodekaschoenos, the territory of the northern Meroitic. The indigenous northern Meroitic population, however, seems to have stayed in place as well. Most main population centers, and even individual houses of the northern Meroitic period continued to be occupied (Trigger 1965). Other sites were smaller and more dispersed, but the population remained sedentary and agriculturally oriented (W.Y. Adams 1977). Although the material culture of the region changed from the northern Meroitic tradition to a new one (named the Ballana culture), craniometric and dental examinations of Meroitic, Ballana and later Christian populations of the Nubian Nile Valley showed strong genetic continuity, suggesting that all three comprised basically the same population (Greene et al. 1972; Greene 1967; Billy 1987). Thus, it would appear that the conquest of the Red Noba was principally a political matter which did not result in any significant population displacement. Life went on in the region much as it had before, only now the population was ruled by Ballana kings (Emery 1938).

The Dodekaschoenos, in turn, fell into the lap of the Blemmyes after the Roman garrisons retreated around AD 289 (Kirwan 1982). For the most part, the population of Dodekaschoenos, who were descended from the northern Meroites and Romans, and who, incidentally, had the same material culture as the Ballana in southern Lower Nubia, remained in place. There is no archaeological evidence for an influx of Blemmye nomads into the valley (Kirwan 1982). Accounts by Olympiodorus (ca. AD 425) speak of a visit to the camp of the Blemmyes chiefs located not in the Nile Valley, but in the desert (Kirwan 1974). Procopius likewise suggests that the Blemmyes were in the desert, not in the riverside towns (Kirwan 1958). Apparently, as in southern Lower Nubia, the sedentary agricultural population of the valley had simply come under the control of a new master, in this case the nomads of the Eastern Desert.[1]

Probably this influx of foreign rulers into Nubia was a result of changes in Rome's foreign policy. Instead of manning the forts in the frontier zone, Rome may have been content to hand over the frontiers to lesser vassals who would be contracted to maintain peace and prosperity, and act as a buffer zone to the Roman Empire (Kirwan 1978, 1982).

But texts of King Silko (Kirwan 1974) indicate that the Noba and Blemmyes competed and even fought against each other. The Noba/Ballana sites south of the Dodekaschoenos were located on the west bank of the river, perhaps in order to afford some protection against the east bank where the Blemmyes nomads were (Triger 1965). Also the Noba/Ballana kings had only Egyptian silver for their royal jewelry; the gold of the Eastern Desert apparently was inaccessible to them (ibid.). As the Kalabsha inscription shows, during the early fifth or sixth century AD the Noba King Silko defeated the Blemmyes in Dodekaschoenos (Kirwan 1974, 1982; W.Y. Adams 1977). Even this conflict may have been part of Rome's attempt to exert some control by playing one client state against another (Kirwan 1974, 1982).

The pattern of hostilities in the North serves to cast doubt on the validity of the conflict theory of nomadism (chapter 1). Records indicate that Dodekaschoeonos was garrisoned by the Romans to keep the Blemmyes nomads at bay. The cessation of hostilities and Rome's withdrawal from Dodekaschoenos in AD 289, however, did not result in "de-nomadization" of the Blemmyes as the conflict theory by implication demands. Olympiodorus clearly states that the Blemmyes nomads did not settle down but stayed in the desert. A similar pattern can be seen in the Middle Nile, concerning the Noba takeover of the Meroitic kingdom.

In the next chapter further conclusions are drawn from the entire sequence discussed to this point. These will illustrate how the symbiosis model provides the closest fit to the archaeologically known nomads of northeast Africa.

Chapter X

Conclusions

As the symbiosis model predicted (chapter 1), in ancient northeast Africa all the known nomadic adaptations developed on the borders of state level societies (Fig. 10.1). There are no reliably documented nomadic pastoral regional populations either in the periods before the development of state level societies, or in areas far removed from the borders of such states. In this respect, the data most closely fit the implications of the symbiosis theory.

The data also fit the symbiosis model insofar as evidence shows that nomad/state relations involved cooperation more often than conflict. Co-operation between the pastoral nomads and agricultural civilizations can be demonstrated in trade between the Naqada III state and the hinterland nomads through the intermediary of the A-Group (chapter 6). Other examples may include the use of Medjay herders by Egyptian nobles during the Twelfth Dynasty; Medjay mercenaries in the Second Intermediate Period (chapter 7); nomad caravaniers on Meroe's overland trade routes; and Ezana's gift of cattle to the Beja (chapter 8).

Conflicts between the state and hinterland nomads are also documented, as between the Medjay and the Middle and New Kingdom Egyptians (chapter 7); the Napatan/Meroitic kingdoms and the Rehreh and Medded nomads on their northeastern frontier; the Axumites and Hagiz nomads of the Southern Atbai (chapter 8); and between the Romans and the Blem-myes of the Eastern Desert (chapter 9). In none of these cases, however, can conflict be seen as the sustaining force of nomadism: relations between the members of each nomad/sedentary pair were also peaceful at times, and included some of the examples of symbiosis presented above. In addition, in some cases conflict can be shown to have resulted in the termination of nomadism (Southern Atbai), while in other cases cessation of hostilities did not result in "de-nomadization," as, for example, among the Blemmyes and the Noba (chapter 9).

To the extent demonstrated above, the northeast African ancient nomads are better explained by the symbiosis model than by the conflict or ecologi-cal model. But there are several caveats. Most obviously, the gaps in the sequence—biased toward the hinterlands as they are—make conclusions

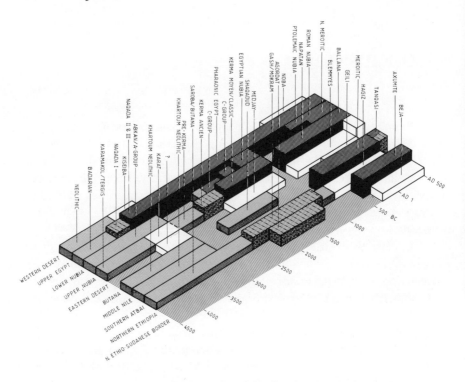

Figure 10.1. Isometric graph of the northeast African archaeological sequences (see also figure 5.2) *Darkest blocks:* agricultural regional populations; *dark gray, pinstriped blocks*: agropastoralists; *light gray blocks*: mixed economy populations; *white blocks*: nomads. *One story high blocks* denote egalitarian societies; *two story blocks* denote ranked societies; *three story blocks* denote state level societies. Note the distribution of white blocks (nomads) on the boundaries of three story high black blocks (agricultural state level societies).

tentative and subject to revision. Second, there are some aspects of the symbiosis model which do not fit the northeast African sequences. Third, as mentioned in the first chapter, the symbiosis explanation leaves some specific aspects such as the actual transition to nomadism unclarified.

The possibly incorrect predictions of the symbiosis model include the proposed developmental trajectory from mixed economy to agropastoralism, and then to either fully agricultural or pastoral adaptations. This predicted trajectory can be documented properly only in the Southern Atbai sequence. Elsewhere, agropastoralism is only weakly documented in two cases, the Naqada I and the Kerma Ancien populations of Egypt and Nubia. In both cases, the populations developed into state level, agricultural societies, and so shed little light on the issue of the agropastoral to nomadic trajectory.

Aside from the problem of documenting nomadism preceded by agropastoralism, however, examples such as the Blemmye and Noba takeover of post-Meroitic Nubia (chapter 9), or even the Medjay takeover of the late Kassala Phase Southern Atbai population (chapters 3, and 7), suggest that a certain form of agropastoralism—nomadic ruling segment with agricultural client group—developed *after* the nomadic adaptation itself. Should this be seen as a devolving level of specialized production from nomadism to agropastoralism, or is there a distinction to be drawn between agropastoralism, as defined in chapter 1, and this clientship form of adaptation?

Perhaps clientship should be seen as a distinct category: a post-symbiosis solution to the nomads' problem of obtaining the needed agricultural products. If nomadism depends on symbiosis with agriculturalists, and if that symbiosis is threatened, nomads may well elect to conquer the agriculturalists and with them the administration of inter-regional trade in order to maintain their own way of life. An historic example of a nomadic takeover for precisely the purpose of maintaining the (nomads') status quo is elegantly portrayed by Salzman in his study of Baluchi nomads (1978).

If this is indeed a general further development of nomad/sedentary relations, the northeast African data sugggest that nomadic conquest does not always result in the conquered/conquering population changing into a bi-segmental agropastoral regional population, with farmer clients as one segment and ruling nomads as the other segment. Under certain conditions, it appears that the conquered client-agricultural segment (the Ballana culture, for example) retained its cultural identity. In such a case, a true agropastoral regional population was apparently not formed since ethnic boundaries between desert and sown were maintained.

In other cases, however, such as the Southern Atbai of the late Kassala Phase, stylistic similarities in ceramics between the Mokram Group and the desert Medjay (Pan-Grave culture) suggest the removal of ethnic boundaries, and thus the creation of a technically agropastoral regional adaptation through takeover by a nomadic population. Unfortunately, the available data are too coarse to allow proper investigation of this interesting dichotomy and its full implications.

Better data are also required for a proper view of the specific aspects of the transformation to nomadism (the third caveat). The symbiosis model has dealt principally with the issue of the maintenance of nomadism. In chapter 1 it was suggested that the immediate historical cause of nomadism, and the precise way in which populations gave up their indigenous adaptation to become nomads could vary widely from time to time and place to place. But is that indeed so? Is there not a general model which can also explain all initial reasons and routes to nomadism?

The currently known northeast African sequences cannot shed much light on this issue. The Kiseiba populations of the fourth millennium BC, for example, may have initially become nomadic for ecological reasons, while conflict may have been responsible in the Eastern Desert (chapter 6). But so could any other specific historic event: there simply are insufficient data to refute any hypothesis.

The same applies to the particular route taken by a regional population to nomadism. The actual transition to nomadism may have taken place over a very short period and in response to very specific historical events (whether cultural or natural). It can only be properly investigated when archaeological remains can be dated more accurately than, say, to the millennium blocks in the Southern Atbai sequence. It also requires a better grasp on historical events in neighboring regions than is now possible in central Sudan and northern Ethiopia.

To this extent, the conclusions drawn from this work are preliminary. The key to the next stage of research on ancient northeast African nomadism seems to lie in the Eastern Desert of Egypt: first, because this region forms the largest and potentially most significant gap in our knowledge of ancient northeast African nomads; second, because the relatively well known history of Egypt's foreign policy and the tight chronologies established for the ancient Nile Valley cultures will provide a much more solid and detailed historic framework for examining the actual transition to nomadism; third, because nomadism has a far longer history in the Eastern Desert—conceivably stretching from as early as the fourth millennium BC to the present (see chapter 6). In the long history of nomadism in the Eastern Desert, it will be possible to isolate and study in more detail the effects of environment and other ecological factors, conflict, symbiosis, and takeovers on the hinterland nomadic adaptation.

Notes

1. For example, it is at least theoretically possible to find nomadic pastoralists in environments so stable and well-suited to the needs of their animals that seasonal migrations become unnecessary. In northeast Africa, however, as in many of the lands that nomads occupy, the environment is not so well-suited: consequently, migrations do take place. Their range, duration, and direction then depend on a combination of local factors: principally, the kinds of animals herded, the distribution of seasonal grazing resources, and the existing political boundaries which hamper or facilitate movement.

2. The particular route to becoming an ethnically distinct nomadic population can, presumably, vary. Some researchers, for example, claim that pastoralists, out of a natural desire for autonomy, split off from a mixed economy population (Lefébure 1979). Others say the split began when agricultural sections in search of new fields, or pastoral sections looking for better pastures, left a tribal territory and eventually became ethnically independent (E. Marx 1978; Gilbert 1983). Another scenario might postulate that a mixed economy or even agropastoral population which found itself within a state administered, regional economic sphere chose to participate as specialized pastoral producers and thus were transformed into a nomadic population.

3. How far away from a state can symbiotic links effect an evolution to nomadic adaptation? The distance logically must have to do with the local terrain and the logistics of contact and of transporting pastoral and agricultural goods, of processing information about market conditions in one or the other economy, and the distance to alternative markets in other agricultural societies. Thus, the distance probably varies depending on local conditions, but only within a set range: one can imagine that beyond a certain point symbiosis is not practical. The exact point can hardly be known, and in any case it probably changed through time. In fact, rather than measuring that point in terms of spatial distance, it may be better to identify it in terms of the number of societal boundaries across which symbiotic links hold. The link can probably best operate when the two sectors of the economy are geographical neighbors. It may also work when a spatially intervening society can act as an intermediary in the exchange of goods between the nomads and the cultivators. Beyond that, however, the presence of more than one intermediate society will probably make symbiosis too costly and unpredictable an endevor, although in theory at least, it would be possible.

CHAPTER 4

1. In further testing, the validity of this pattern seemed compromised because overlaying the same concentric circles on period 3 settlements produced somewhat

similar clustering. But perhaps, as is shown further on in the text, the similar clustering in period 3 gives an indication of a sizeable herding segment operating at that time, as well.

2. The low density sites—short term occupations—are peppered across the survey zone without regard to proxemic rules. They are not positioned with any regularity relative to other low density sites, or to high and medium density ones. This is to be expected for sites only temporarily occupied.

3. It will be noted that the three clusters of three or four sites each located in the Sharab el Gash fit into this catchment pattern only on the assumption that all three or four sites within each cluster were part of one settlement. The marked ceramic stylistic similarities within each site cluster support this assumption (Sadr, ms.). The site clusters may represent one of three things. First, it is possible that the sites within each cluster actually formed a single community like the neighborhoods of the Qemant (Gamst 1969) or the dispersed Nuer villages (Jackson 1923). Second, it is possible that one site in the cluster was the parent village, while the others were offspring communities established later. Third, it is possible that the sites in the clusters were consecutively occupied: a case of horizontal stratigraphy. No matter which model fits best, if only the central site of each cluster is chosen, they can be neatly fitted into the proxemics pattern.

4. The southernmost of the three period 2 centers in Figure 4.8 shows three medium density sites close together. The other two centers are each a high density, large village settlement. The primacy of the southernmost center's medium density sites over the ring of other medium density sites at 5 km radius is better seen in the map showing site distribution by size. The ceramics of the two main sites in the southernmost cluster, SEGs 7 and 14, are stylistically very similar, suggesting the possibility that the two sites were actually one community. The two may have been related in one of the three ways described in note 3 above.

5. Strangely enough, the ceramics of the Hagiz Group do not stylistically resemble the ceramics of the preceding Mokram Group, but rather those of the Gash Group of period 2: in other words, the indigenous style of the Southern Atbai before the cultural takeover by the Medjay (see chapters 3 and 7). The stylistic change seems a significant clue for explaining the actual transformation to nomadism around 750 BC, but its meaning continues to elude me.

CHAPTER 8

1. It has been argued that the repopulation of Nubia was made possible by the use of the saqqia irrigation technology (W.Y. Adams 1977; Firth 1915; Trigger 1965).

CHAPTER 9

1. The disjunction between the presence of only one archaeological culture (the Ballana) but of textual references to two peoples in Nubia at this time (the Noba and the Blemmyes) has led to long drawn discussions about the so-called "X-Group problem" (after Reisner's original term for the Ballana culture) (Monneret de Villard 1938; Emery 1938; Trigger 1969; Kirwan 1982; W.Y. Adams 1977,1982, among

others). It would seem that there need not be any contradictions between the archaeology and the texts. The latter speak of the ruling strata of society, of which there were two: the Noba and the Blemmyes. The archaeology, however, deals with the material culture of the population of Nubia, all of whom were simply the post-Meroitic residents of the area.

Appendices

Appendix 1. Three Examples of the Pastoral Classification

Goldschmidt's classification (1979)

A. Large stock, flat land nomads, who are either
   (1) mounted, or
   (2) pedestrian.
   In each category, they are either
       (a) independent of agriculture, or
       (b) integrated with agriculture, or
       (c) practicing secondary agriculture.
B. Small stock mountain dwelling transhumants, who are either
   (a), (b), or (c), as in the above case.

Khazanov's classification (1984)

1. Pastoral nomadism proper, without any agriculture, highly mobile, possess riding animals.
2. Semi-nomadic pastoralism, rely extensively on pastoralism, also engage in agriculture as a secondary subsistence measure. There are two varieties here;
   (a) those societies wherein each household engages in both agriculture and pastoralism, and
   (b) those societies which have specialized sections attending to agriculture or pastoralism.
3. Semi-sedentary pastoralism, where agriculture is the predominant economic activity. This type also has the variants (a) and (b).

4. Herdsman husbandry, where most of the population is sedentary, and specialist herders take care of the stock.
5. Yaylagh pastoralism, or transhumant pastoralists whose use of different vertically separated ecological zones in mountainous terrain sets them apart from the lowland free range herders. Otherwise, the characteristics of the transhumants may be like types 2, 3, or 4.
6. Sedentary animal husbandry where agriculture is by far the most important economic activity. This type refers essentially to farmers who keep some stock.

Cribb's classification (1982)

	Productive regime	Number of stock	Marketing strategy	Mobility
Type 1.	Fully specialized agriculture, minimal pastoralism	A few animals for traction and transport	Agricultural products marketed and subsistence	Fully sedentary
Type 2.	Predominantly farming, limited pastoralism	Small number of stock for household needs	Agricultural, subsistence pastoralism	Sedentary, limited movement of flock around village
Type 3.	Pastoralism combined with cultivation	Numbers beyond perennial carrying capacity of locality	Agricultural and pastoral products marketed	Village-based transhumance
Type 4.	Predominantly or exclusively pastoral	Large numbers of stock well beyond carrying capacity of locality	Pastoral products marketed. Subsistence cultivation optional	Fully nomadic

Appendix 2. Early Kassala Phase Site Data

Table App. 2.1. Butana Group Dates

Site	Level	C14 date (BP)	MASCA cal.	Lab no.
KG 7	16	4,421 ± 93	3,163 BC	SMU 1156
KG 7	16	4,569 ± 68	3,351 BC	SMU 1151
KG 23a	18	4,542 ± 253	3,319 BC	SMU 1155
KG 23c	17	5,460 ± 130	4,372 BC	SMU 1194
KG 23c	23	4,519 ± 67	3,283 BC	SMU 1188
KG 23c	27	4,727 ± 154	3,544 BC	SMU 1201
KG 96	lowest	2,755 ± 107	984 BC	SMU 1187
N 125	?	4,410 ± 90	3,152 BC	Tx 445

Table App. 2.2. Butana Group Sites

Site	Size (ha)	Depth (cm)	Surface artifact density	Total area excavated (m²)	Old no.	Comment
KG 1	0.3	35	High	2	N101 (?)	
KG 5	4.5	40	High	2		
KG 7	8.8	85	High	4	N107	
KG 23	10.2	150	High	11	N123	
KG 29	2.5	40	High	5	N129	Disturbed
KG 50	4.2	0	Low	0	—	Lithic scatter
KG 56	<1.0	0	Low	0	—	Mixed site
KG 96	7.0	75	High	3	—	
N 125	<1.0	100	High	1	N125	Pottery kiln (?)

Table App. 2.3. Butana Group Faunal Remains (Peters 1986)

Site	KG 7 n	KG 7 %	KG 23 n	KG 23 %	KG 29 N n	KG 29 N %	KG 29 S n	KG 29 S %
FISH	20	33.8	9	3.3	7	4.0	26	28.6
REPTILES	19	32.2	110	40.9	7	4.0	17	18.7
BIRDS	6	10.2	5	1.9	—	—	—	—
WILD MAMMALS	13	22.1	57	21.2	28	15.8	6	6.6
Primates	—	—	1	0.4	—	—	—	—
Lagomorpha	—	—	2	0.7	—	—	—	—
Rodentia	—	—	1	0.4	—	—	—	—
Carnivora	1	1.7	16	5.9	1	0.6	1	1.1
Tubulidentata	—	—	3	1.1	—	—	—	—
Artiodactyla	—	—	34	12.7	27	15.2	—	—
Suids	—	—	3	1.1	1	0.6	—	—
Hippopotamus	—	—	—	—	2	1.1	1	1.1
Small antelopes	7	11.9	8	3.0	8	4.5	—	—
Medium antelopes	5	8.5	18	6.7	11	6.1	3	3.3
Large antelopes	—	—	5	1.9	4	2.3	1	1.1
V. Large antelopes	—	—	—	—	1	0.6	—	—
DOMESTIC MAMMALS	1	1.7	9	3.3	63	35.6	9	9.9
Artiodactyla	—	—	9	3.3	—	—	—	—
Small livestock	—	—	6	2.2	14	7.9	5	5.5
Cattle	1	1.7	3	1.1	49	27.7	4	4.4
WILD OR DOMESTIC MAMMALS	—	—	79	29.4	72	40.7	33	36.3
Carnivora	—	—	12	4.5	2	1.1	5	5.5
Artiodactyla	—	—	67	24.9	70	39.6	28	20.8
Small bovid	—	—	16	5.9	12	6.8	12	13.2
Large bovid	—	—	44	16.4	58	32.8	16	17.6
Bovidae *indet.*	—	—	7	2.6	—	—	—	—
TOTALS	59	100.0	269	100.0	177	100.0	91	100.0

Appendix 3. Gash Group Sites

Table App. 3.1. C14 Dates from Mahal Teglinos (Fattovich and Vitagliano 1989)

Level (5 cm)	Date	Calibrated range 2 SD (Klein 1982)	Material	Lab no.
13–15	3780 ± 90 bp	2535–1950 BC	charcoal	Gif 7651
23–24	4010 ± 90 bp	2885–2310 BC	charcoal	Gif 7652
ca. 30	3860 ± 60 bp	2545–2160 BC	charcoal	??
32–33	3980 ± 280 bp	3350–1870 BC	charcoal	Gif 7653
40	4220 ± 90 bp	3150–2555 BC	charcoal	Gif 7654

Table App. 3.2. Gash Group Site Data

Site no.	Size (ha)	Depth of deposits (cm)	Surface artifact density	No. of artifact concentrations
KG 52	1.2	0	Medium	2 major, few minor
KG 53	0.5	0	Low	—
KG 93	1.7	5–10	Medium	not recorded
JAG 1	12	>100	High	3 very major
AG 1	0.5	0–5	Low	—
AG 2	0.3	0–5	Medium	not recorded
EG 1	0.9	0–10	Medium	3 major, few minor
EG 4	0.7	0–5	Medium	1 major
SEG 2	1.9	0–5	Medium	few
SEG 7	7.6	5–10	Medium	6 major
SEG 10	0.2	0–5	Medium	few
SEG 14	7.2	5–10	Medium	7 major
SEG 16	3.0	0–5	Medium	8
SEG 19	3.9	0–5	Medium	1 major
SEG 20	0.5	0–5	Medium	not recorded
SEG 21	3.0	0–5	Medium	3
SEG 22	1.7	0–5	Low	—
JE 2	< 1	n.r.	n.r.	not recorded
SEG 37	1.5	5–10	Medium	3
SEG 39	3.1	n.r.	Medium	few
SEG 51	1.8	n.r.	Medium	4
SEG 55	0.5	—	Low	—
SEG 56	8.5	>50	High	1 major
SEG 59	2.6	n.r	Medium	4
SEG 64	0.4	0	Low	3 minor
SEG 65	0.3	n.r.	Medium	1
SEG 66	1.0	0	Low	3 minor
K 1	11.0	>200	High	1 major
K 2	< 1	?	n.a.	Burials only
K 4	1.8	0	Low	Among boulders

Table App. 3.3. Wealth of Ceramic Design Variety on Gash Group Sites with Over 30 Sherds Collected.

Site no.	Number of ceramic design types	Total sample of sherds collected
Mahal Teglinos	9	36
SEG 56	8	118
JAG 1	7	38
SEG 14	4	37
SEG 7	4	31
KG 52	3	33
KG 93	3	30
SEG 19	3	37
JE 2	3	58
K7	2	55
SEG 59	2	36
SEG 64	2	45

Appendix 4. Mokram Group Data

Table App. 4.1. Mokram Group Sites

Site	Size (ha)	Depth (cm)	Density	Site	Size (ha)	Depth (cm)	Density
GS 4	1.0	10	Medium	KG 51	0.9	0	Low
JAG 1	8.0	?	High	KG 52	0.9	0	Medium
T 1	1.4	5	Medium	KG 88	1.5	0	Low
EG 2	0.5	5	Medium	KG 97	1.2	0	Low
EG 3	1.5	5	Medium	KG 98	1.3	0	Low
EG 4	0.7	5	Medium	KG 101	0.7	0	Low
SEG 1	0.5	0	Low	KG 102	1.3	10	Medium
SEG 2	1.9	5	Medium	KG 108	1.0	0	Low
SEG 4	1.2	5	Medium	KG 123	3.0	10	Medium
SEG 5	0.6	0	Medium	KG 124	1.0	5	Medium
SEG 7	7.6	5	Medium	KG 125	0.7	0	Low
SEG 8	0.7	5	Medium	KG 128	1.0	0	Low
SEG 14	7.2	5	Medium	KG 130	0.7	0	Low
SEG 17	1.3	5	Medium	KG 42	1.5	0	Medium
SEG 18	0.9	5	Low	KG 122	1.0	0	Low
SEG 19	3.9	5	Medium	KG 43	1.0	5	Medium
SEG 27	3.0	0	Low	KG 95	1.2	5	Medium
SEG 32	0.8	0	Low	KG 38	1.0	0	Medium
SEG 40	2.6	5	Medium	KG 121	0.9	0	Low
SEG 46	1.5	5	Medium	EG 1	0.9	5	Medium
SEG 47	1.8	5	Medium	SEG 6	1.0	0	Medium
SEG 48	1.6	0	Medium	SEG 52	0.6	0	Low
SEG 50	0.1	0	Low	K 18	3.7	0	Medium
SEG 53	3.0	0	Medium	KG 53	0.5	0	Low
SEG 54	0.6	0	Medium	KG 109	1.8	5	Medium
SEG 61	4.9	0	Medium	AG 1	0.5	0	Low
K 1	4.0	60	High	SEG 28	2.2	0	Low
K 2	?	?	Burials	SEG 34	1.0	0	Low
K 10	6.2	5	Medium	SEG 35	2.4	5	Medium
K 19	2.8	5	Medium	SEG 39	3.1	0	Burials
K 20	2.6	0	Medium	SEG 49	1.2	0	Low
K 27	1.0	5	Medium	SEG 60	0.6	5	Medium
KG 2	0.4	0	Low	SEG 64	0.4	0	Low
KG 3	3.1	0	Low	KG 56	<1.0	0	Low
KG 4	0.2	0	Low	KG 85	0.1	0	Medium
KG 6	0.8	0	Low	KG 86	0.3	0	Low
KG 11	0.2	0	Low	KG 87	0.1	0	Low
KG 20	3.0	10	Medium	KG 107	0.5	0	Low
KG 25	3.0	0	Low				

Table App. 4.1 (cont.)

Late Mokram Group sites and components

GS 4	<1.0	?	Low	SEG 17	<1.0	?	Low
SEG 9	0.6	?	Medium	SEG 19	<1.0	?	Low
SEG 10	0.2	?	Medium	SEG 21	<1.0	?	Low
SEG 12	0.9	?	Medium	KG 102	<1.0	?	Low
SEG 13	0.9	?	Medium	KG 124	<1.0	?	Low
SEG 14	<1.0	?	Medium (?)	EG 4	<1.0	?	Low

Table App. 4.2. Mokram Group Faunal Remains (from Peters 1986)

Faunal remains	*KG 20*	*KG 124*
Giraffe	—	1
Small antelope	1	—
Cattle	1	1
Wild ass or donkey	1	—
Small bovid (domestic ?)	4	—
Large bovid (domestic ?)	1	—
Total number of identified vertebrate specimens	8	2

Table App. 4.3. Distribution of Period 3 Earthen Mounds

Site	*No. of mounds*	*Site*	*No. of mounds*	*Site*	*No. of mounds*
EG1	1	K19	2	KG95	1
SEG27	1	K20	1	KG97	1
SEG32	1	KG2	1	KG98	1
SEG34	1	KG3	1	KG107	1
SEG35	1	KG6	1	KG109	1
SEG48	2	KG42	1	KG121	1
SEG52	1	KG43	1	KG122	1
SEG53	3	KG52	1	KG123	1
SEG61	1	KG53	1	KG124	2
SEG64	1	KG85	1	KG125	1
K10	6	KG86	2	KG128	1
K18	1	KG88	1	KG130	1

Table App. 4.4. Distribution of Earthen Mounds by Ecological Zones

Ecological zone	Percentage of sites with mounds (N=36)
Arable (primary)	5.5
(secondary)	13.8
(tertiary)	52.7
Steppe	27.7

Table App. 4.5. Wealth of Ceramic Design Variety on Classic Mokram Group Sites with Sample Sizes over 50

Site no.	Total number of ceramic design types	Total number of sherds collected
JAG 1	30	116
Mahal Teglinos (K 1)	21	163
KG 20	15	117
K19	12	80
SEG 14	10	54
KG 124	10	166
KG 109	9	62
KG 123	9	131
SEG 17	8	53
SEG 40	8	75
SEG 47	8	126
SEG 53	8	56
KG 42	7	53
KG 53	6	63
KG 102	6	79
GS 4	5	71
SEG 46	5	74
KG 85	5	50
SEG 48	4	59
SEG 54	3	52

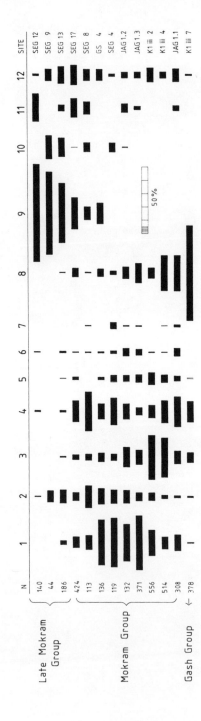

Figure App. 4.1. Seriation of ceramic types from selected period 2–3 sites: Type 1. Typical Mokram Group net patterned cross-incised; Type 2. Groove-carved; Type 3. Mokram Group fine red slipped; Type 4. Mineral tempered plain; Type 5. Wiped plain; Type 6. Complex impressed and incised; Type 7. Punctate; Type 8. Mineral tempered scraped; Type 9. Late Mokram fiber tempered with cross-incised rim band; Type 10. Mat-impressed; Type 11. Hagiz Group pink fiber tempered; Type 12. Varia.

Appendix 5. Hagiz Group Data

Table App. 5.1. Hagiz Group Sites

Site	Size (ha)	Density	Site	Size (ha)	Density
JE 1	1.8	Low	K 15	0.1	Low
JE 2	<1.0	Low	K 16	12.6	Low
AG 1	<1.0	Low	K 17	3.3	Low
EG 3	<1.0	Low	KG 2	<1.0	Low
EG 4	<1.0	Low	KG 3	ca 2.0	Low
SEG 1	<1.0	Low	KG 4	<1.0	Low
SEG 2	<1.0	Low	KG 6	<1.0	Low
SEG 5	<1.0	Low	KG 30	1.6	Low
SEG 6	<1.0	Low	KG 34	0.2	Low
SEG 8	<1.0	Low	KG 35	0.08	Low
SEG 17	<1.0	Low	KG 36	0.1	Low
SEG 20	<1.0	Low	KG 37	<1.0	Low
SEG 21	<1.0	Low	KG 39	0.2	Low
SEG 25	3.0	Low	KG 41	0.7	Low
SEG 27	<1.0	Low	KG 45	0.08	Low
SEG 28	<1.0	Low	KG 48	0.005	Low
SEG 34	<1.0	Low	KG 53	<1.0	Low
SEG 36	2.2	Low	KG 81	2.2	Medium
SEG 42	<1.0	Low	KG 83	0.09	Low
SEG 43	<1.0	Low	KG 88	<1.0	Low
SEG 45	<1.0	Low	KG 89	<1.0	Low
SEG 52	<1.0	Low	KG 92	<1.0	Low
SEG 55	<1.0	Low	KG 97	<1.0	Low
SEG 61	<1.0	Low	KG 98	1.3	Low
SEG 62	0.5	Low	KG 100	4.0	Low
SEG 63	1.1	Low	KG 101	<1.0	Low
SEG 64	<1.0	Low	KG 107	<1.0	Low
K 1	ca 2.0	Low	KG 109	<1.0	Low
K 2	1.5	Low	KG 110	1.3	Low
K 4	ca 4.0	Low	KG 111	7.5	Low
K 6	5.2	Low	KG 116	0.8	Medium
K 7	<1.0	Low	KG 118	<1.0	Low
K 9	3.7	Low	KG 123N	1.0	Medium
K 10	<1.0	Low	KG 127	<1.0	Low
K 14	1.0	Low	KG 128	<1.0	Low

Table App. 5.2. Distribution of Grinding Stones on Single Component Period 4
Sites

Site	Grinding stones	Site	Grinding stones	Site	Grinding stones
SEG 25	−				
SEG 36	−	K 17	−	KG 48	−
SEG 62	−	KG 30	+	KG 81	−
SEG 63	−	KG 34	−	KG 83	−
K 6	+	KG 35	+	KG 100	−
K 9	−	KG 36	+	KG 110	−
K 14	−	KG 39	+	KG 111	−
K 15	−	KG 41	−	KG 116	−
K 16	−	KG 45	−	JE 1	−

+ few   − absent

Bibliography

Adams, R. McC.
1974   "The Mesopotamian Social Landscape: A View from the Fron-
        tier." In C.B. Moore, ed., *Reconstructing Complex Societies*. Sup-
        plement to the Bulletin of the American Schools of Oriental
        Research no. 20, Cambridge, Mass., 1–11.

Adams, W.Y.
1977   *Nubia: Corridor to Africa*. London: Allen Lane.
1979   "Kush and the Peoples of Northeast Africa." *Meroitica* 5: 9–15.
1982   "Meroitic Textual Material from Qasr Ibrim." *Meroitica* 6: 211–
        217.

Adams, W.Y., and H-Å. Nordström
1963   "The Archaeological Survey on the West Bank of the Nile:
        Third Season, 1961–62." *Kush* 11: 10–46.

Adamson, D.A., F. Gasse, F.A. Street, and M.A.J. Williams
1980   "Late Quaternary History of the Nile." *Nature* 287(5786): 50–55.

Addison, F.
1949   *Jebel Moya*. London: Oxford University Press.
1956   "Second Thoughts on Jebel Moya." *Kush* 4: 4–19.

Ali, (Hakem) A.M.
1972   "Meroitic Settlement of the Butana (Central Sudan)." In P.J.
        Ucko, R. Tringham, and G.W. Dimbleby, eds., *Man, Settlement
        and Urbanism*. Cambridge, Mass.: Schenkman, 639–646.

Amin El-Tom, M.
1975   *The Rains of the Sudan*. Khartoum: Khartoum University Press.

Anfray, F.
1963   "Une campagne de fouilles à Yeha (février–mars, 1960)." *An-
        nales d'Ethiopie* 5:171–232.
1965   "Notes sur quelques poteries Axoumites." *Annales d'Ethiopie* 6:
        217–220.
1967   "Matara." *Annales d'Ethiopie* 7: 33–53.
1968   "Aspects de l'archéologie éthiopienne." *Journal of African His-
        tory* 9(3): 345–366.

1970   "Notes archéologiques." *Annales d'Ethiopie* 8: 31–56.

1972   "L'archéologie d'Axoum en 1972." *Paideuma* 17: 60–78.

Anfray, F., and G. Annequin

1965   "Matara: deuxième, troisième et quatrième campagnes de fouilles." *Annales d'Ethiopie* 6: 49–142.

Arbos, P.

1923   "The Geography of Pastoral Life: Illustrated with European Examples." *The Geographical Review* 13(4): 559–575.

Arkell, A.J.

1949   *Early Khartoum*. London: Oxford University Press.

1950   "Varia Sudanica." *Journal of Egyptian Archaeology* 36: 24–40.

1953   *Shaheinab*. London: Oxford University Press.

1954   "Four Occupation Sites at Agordat." *Kush* 2: 23–63.

1961   *A History of the Sudan from the Earliest Times to 1821*. London: Athlone Press.

Arkell, A.J., and P.J. Ucko

1965   "Review of Predynastic Development in the Nile Valley." *Current Anthropology* 6: 145–166.

Asad, T.

1970   *The Kababish Arabs: Power, Authority and Consent in a Nomadic Tribe*. New York: Praeger.

1979   "Equality in Nomadic Social Systems? Notes Towards the Dissolution of an Anthropological Category." In *Pastoral Production and Society* (1979), 419–428.

Bacon, C.R.K.

1922   "The Anuak." *Sudan Notes and Records* 5: 113–129.

Bacon, E.

1954   "Types of Pastoral Nomadism in Central and Southwest Asia." *Southwestern Journal of Anthropology* 10(1): 44–68.

Baker, J., and D. Brothwell

1980   *Animal Diseases in Archaeology*. New York: Academic Press.

Baker, Sir Samuel White

1967   *The Nile Tributaries of Abyssinia*. London: Macmillan.

Banks, K.M.

1984   *Climates, Cultures and Cattle: The Holocene Archaeology of the Eastern Sahara*. New Delhi: Pauls Press.

ms.   Flaked Stone Lithic Technology in the Southern Atbai: Mokram and Hagiz Group Assemblages. To be published by Southern Methodist University Press as part of the Butana Archaeological Project final reports.

Barbour, K.M.

1964   *The Republic of the Sudan: A Regional Geography.* London: University of London Press.

Barker, G.

1981   *Landscape and Society: Prehistoric Central Italy.* London and New York: Academic Press.

Barth, F.

1961   *Nomads of South Persia: The Basseri Tribe of the Khamseh Confederacy.* Universities Ethnographiske Museum. Bulletin 8. Oslo: Universitetsforlaget.

1962   "Nomadism in the Mountain and Plateau Areas of Southwest Asia." In *The Problems of the Arid Zone: Nomadic Pastoralism as a Method of Land Use. Arid Zone Researches—XVIII. Proceedings of the Paris Symposium,* pp. 341–355. Paris.

1973   "A General Perspective on Nomad-Sedentary Relations in the Middle East." In C.M. Nelson, ed., *The Desert and the Sown.* Berkeley: University of California Press, 11–21.

Bates, D.G.

1971   "The Role of the State in Peasant-Nomad Mutualism." *Anthropological Quarterly* 44(3): 109–131.

Bates, D.G., and S.H. Lees

1977   "The Role of Exchange in Productive Specialization." *American Anthropologist* 79(4): 824–841.

Baumgartel, E.J.

1970   *Petrie's Naqada Excavation; A Supplement.* London: Quaritch.

Behrensmeyer, A.K., and A.P. Hill

1980   *Fossils in the Making.* Chicago: University of Chicago Press.

Bernard, A., and N. Lacroix

1906   *L'évolution du nomadisme en Algérie.* Alger: A. Jourdan.

Bietak, M.

1966   *Ausgrabungen in Sayala-Nubien 1961–1965: Denkmäler der C-Gruppe und der Pan-Gräber-Kultur.* Österreichische Akademie der Wissenschaften, Philosophisch-historische Klasse, Denkschriften 92. Vienna: Hermann Böhlaus Nachf.

1968   *Studien zur Chronologie der Nubischen C-Gruppe.* Österreichische Akademie der Wissenschaften, Philosophisch-historische Klasse, Denkschriften 97. Vienna: Hermann Böhlaus Nachf.

1986   "The C-Group and the Pan-Grave Culture in Nubia." *Sixth International Conference for Nubian Studies, Prepublication of Main Papers,* vol. 1. Klassik Institutt, University of Bergen.

Billy, G.

1987   "La population de la nécropole d'Abri-Misimina." *Archéologie du Nil Moyen,* 2: 121–141.

Binford, L. R.

1978   *Nunamiut Ethnoarchaeology.* New York: Academic Press.

1981   *Bones: Ancient Man and Modern Myths.* New York: Academic Press.

Blackman, A.M.

1914   *The Rock Tombs of Meir, Part I.* The Archaeological Survey of Egypt, memoir no. 22. London.

1915a   *The Rock Tombs of Meir, Part II.* The Archaeological Survey of Egypt, memoir no. 23. London.

1915b   *The Rock Tombs of Meir, Part III.* The Archaeological Survey of Egypt, memoir no. 24. London.

Bonnet, C., B. Privati, C. Simon, and L. Chaix

1982   "Kerma, Soudan 1981–1982." *Genava* 30: 1–59.

Bonnet, C., N. Ferrero, C. Simon, L. Chaix, and Salah M. Ahmed

1984   "Kerma, Soudan 1982–1984." *Genava* 32: 5–42.

Bonnet, C., B. Privati, C. Simon, L. Chaix, and P. De Paepe

1986   "Kerma, Soudan 1984–1986." *Genava* 34: 5–45.

Bonnet, C., B. Privati, C. Simon, L. Chaix, and P. De Paepe

1988   "Kerma, Soudan 1986–1987—1987–1988." *Genava* 36: 5–35.

Bonte, P.

1981   "Ecological and Economic Factors in the Determination of Pastoral Specialization." *Journal of Asian and African Studies* 16(1/2): 33–49.

Bower, J.R.F., C.M. Nelson, A.F. Waibel, and S. Wandibba

1977   "The University of Massachusetts Later Stone Age/Pastoral 'Neolithic' Comparative Study in Central Kenya: An Overview." *Azania* 12: 119–146.

Bradley, R.J.

1984   "Meroitic Chronology." *Meroitica* 7: 195–212.

1986　"A Model for Pastoralism in the Meroitic Butana." In M. Krause, ed., *Nubische Studien*. Mainz a. R.: Ph. von Zabern, 25–31.

Braidwood, R.J.

1960　"The Agricultural Revolution." *Scientific American*, September 1960.

Braudel, F.

1973　*The Mediterranean and the Mediterranean World of Phillip II*. New York: William Collin's Sons, Ltd. and Harper and Row.

Breasted, J.H.

1906　*Ancient Records of Egypt*, vol. I. Chicago: Chicago University Press.

Brunton, G.

1932　"The Predynastic Town-site at Hierakonpolis." In *Studies Presented to F.Ll. Griffith*. London, 272–276.

1937　*Mostagedda and the Tasian Culture*. London: Bernard Quaritch Ltd.

1947　*Matmar*. London.

Brunton, G., and G. Caton-Thompson

1928　*The Badarian Civilisation*. London: Quaritch.

Butzer, K.W.

1959　"Environment and Human Ecology during Predynastic and Early Dynastic Times." *Bulletin de la Société Géographique Egypte* 32: 43–87.

1960　"Archaeology and Geology in Ancient Egypt." *Science* 132 (3440): 1617–1624.

1974　"Modern Egyptian Pottery Clays and Predynastic Buffware." *Journal of Near Eastern Studies* 23: 377–382.

1975　"Patterns of Environmental Change in the Near East During Late Pleistocene and early Holocene Times." In F. Wendorf and A.E. Marks, eds., *Problems in Prehistory: North Africa and the Levant*. Dallas, Tex.: Southern Methodist University Press, 389–404.

1976　*Early Hydraulic Civilisation in Egypt*. Chicago: University of Chicago Press.

1980　"The Holocene Lake Plain of North Rudolf, East Africa." *Physical Geography* 1(1): 42–58.

1982　"Empires, Capitals and Landscapes of Ancient Ethiopia." *Archaeology* 35(5): 30–38.

Caneva, I.

1983   *Pottery Using Gatherers and Hunters at Saggai (Sudan): Preconditions for Food Production.* Origini XII. Rome.

1984   "Meroitic Graves at Geili." Paper read at the Fifth International Conference for Meroitic Studies, Rome.

1985a   "La necropoli di Geili." *La ricerca scientifica* 112:371–392.

1985b   "The Prehistory of Central Sudan: Hints for an Overview." In *Studi di paletnologia in onore di Salvatore M. Puglisi.* University of Rome, 425–432.

1988   "Late Neolithic to Recent Graves at Geili." In I. Caneva, ed., *El Geili: The History of a Middle Nile Environment.* Cambridge Monographs in Archaeology 29. British Archaeological Reports International Series 424, pp. 151–227.

Capot-Rey, R.

1953   *Le Sahara français.* Paris: Presses Universitaires de France.

Carlson, R.L.

1966   "A Neolithic Site in the Murshid District, Nubia." *Kush* 14: 53–62.

Chang, C., and H.A. Koster

1986   "Beyond Bones: Toward an Archaeology of Pastoralism." In M.B. Schiffer, ed., *Advances in Archaeological Method and Theory,* Vol. 9. New York: Academic Press, 97–148.

Chaplin, R.E.

1969   "The Use of Non-Morphological Criteria in the Study of Animal Domestication from Bones Found on Archaeological Sites." In P.J. Ucko and G.W.Dimbleby, eds., *The Domestication and Exploitation of Plants and Animals.* Chicago: Aldine Press, 231–245.

1971   *The Study of Animal Bones from Archaeological Sites.* New York: Seminar Press.

Chittick, N.

1974   "Excavations at Aksum, 1973–4: A Preliminary Report." *Azania* 9: 159–205.

Claessen, H.J.M.

1981   "Reaching for the Moon? Some Problems and Prospects of Cultural Evolutionism." In S.E. van der Leeuw, ed., *Archaeological Approaches to the Study of Complexity.* Amsterdam: University of Amsterdam Press, 15–41.

Clark, J.D.
1970   *The Prehistory of Africa*. London: Thames and Hudson.
Clark, J.D., M.A.J. Williams, and A.B. Smith
1973   "The Geomorphology and Archaeology of Adrar Bous, Central Sahara: A Preliminary Report." *Quaternaria* 17: 245–297.
Clark, J.D., and A. Stemler
1975   "Early Domesticated Sorghum from Central Sudan." *Nature* 254: 588–59
Cohen, R.
1978   "Introduction." In R. Cohen and E. R. Service, eds., *The Origins of the State*. Philadelphia: Institute for the Study of Human Issues, 1–21.
Coltorti, M., A. D'Alessandro, R. Fattovich, P. Lenoble, and K. Sadr
1984   "Gash Delta Archaeological Project: 1984 Field Season." *Nyame Akuma* 24/25: 20–23.
Collier, S., and J.P. White
1976   "Get Them Young? Age and Sex Inferences on Animal Domestication in Archaeology." *American Antiquity* 41: 96–101.
Connor, D.
1984   "The Kiseiba Plateau and Bir Murr Playa." In Wendorf, Schild, and Close (1984), *Cattle-Keepers of the Eastern Sahara*, 350–404.
Coon, C.S.
1943   "Southern Arabia, a Problem for the Future." In *Studies in the Anthropology of Oceania, and Asia*. Papers of the Peabody Museum of American Archaeology and Ethnology, Harvard University no. 20. Cambridge, Mass, 187–220.
Coppa, A., and A.M. Palmieri
1988   "Changing Dietary Patterns at Geili." In I. Caneva, ed., *El Geili: The History of a Middle Nile Environment*. Cambridge Monographs in Archaeology 29. British Archaeological Reports International Series 424, pp. 275–303.
Cossar, B.
1945   "Necropoli precristiana di Seleclaca." In C. Conti-Rossini, ed., *Studi Etiopici*. Rome.
Courtin, J.
1966   "Le Néolithique du Bourkou, Nord-Tchad." *L'Anthropologie* 70(3–4): 269–282.
Costantini, L., R. Fattovich, and M. Piperno

1982   "Preliminary Report of Archaeological Investigations at the Site of Mahal Teglinos (Kassala) November 1981." *Nyame Akuma* 21: 30–33.

Costantini, L., R. Fattovich, M. Piperno, and K. Sadr

1983   "Gash Delta Archaeological Project: 1982 Field Season." *Nyame Akuma* 23: 17–19.

Cremaschi, M., A. D'Alessandro, R. Fattovich, and M. Piperno

1986   "Gash Delta Archaeological Project: 1985 Field Season." *Nyame Akuma* 27: 42–45.

Cribb, R.

1984   "Greener Pastures: Mobility, Migration and the Pastoral Mode of Subsistence." *Production pastorale et société* 14: 11–46.

Cumming, D.C.

1937   "The History of Kassala and the Province of Taka." *Sudan Notes and Records* 20: 1–63.

Cunnison, I.

1966   *Baggara Arabs: Power and Lineage in a Sudanese Nomad Tribe.* Oxford: Clarendon Press.

D'Alessandro, A.

1985   "Indagini preliminari sulla ceramica protostorica del sito di Mahal Teglinos nel delta del Gash (Sudan Orientale)." Unpublished thesis, Istituto Universitario Orientale di Napoli.

D'Andrea, A.C., and Y. Tsubakisaka

1990   "Plant Remains Preserved in Kassala Phase Ceramics, Eastern Sudan." *Nyame Akuma* 33: 16.

Davis, S.J.

1984   "The Advent of Milk and Wool Production in Western Iran: Some Speculations." In J. Clutton-Brock and C. Grigson, eds., *Animals and Archaeology,* Vol. 3, *Early Herders and Their Flocks.* British Archaeological Reports, International Series, 202, 265–278.

Demicheli, A.M.

1976   *Rapporti di pace e di guerra dell' Egitto Romano con le popolazioni dei Deserti Africani.* Milan: Giuffré Editore.

DeMorgan, J.

1897   *Recherches sur les origines de l'Egypte: Ethnographie préhistorique et le tombeau royal de Nagadah.* Paris: Leroux.

DeMorgan, J., V. Bouriant, G. Legrain, G. Jequier, and A. Brasanti

1894   *Catalogues des monuments et inscriptions de l' Egypte antique. Ier séries: Haute Egypte*. Tôme Ier de la Frontière de Nubie à Kom Ombos. Vienna.

Dickson, H.R.P.

1951   *The Arab of the Desert. A Glimpse into Badawin Life in Kuwait and Sa'udi Arabia*. London: George Allen and Unwin Ltd.

Dombrowski, J.C.

1972   *Excavations in Ethiopia: Lalibela and Natchabiet Caves, Begemder Province*. Ph.D. dissertation. Ann Arbor: University Microfilms International.

Donadoni, S., and S. Bosticco

1982   "Scavi italiani al Gebel Barkal." *Meroitica* 6: 291–302.

Driberg, J.H.

1922   "Preliminary Account of the Didinga." *Sudan Notes and Records* 5: 208–222.

Durante, S., R. Fattovich, and M. Piperno

1980   "Archaeological Survey of the Gash Delta, Kassala Province." *Nyame Akuma* 17: 64–71.

Dyson-Hudson, N.

1972   "The Study of Nomads." *Journal of Asian and African Studies* 7(1/2): 2–29.

Dyson-Hudson, R.

1972   "Pastoralism: Self-Image and Behavioral Reality." *Journal of Asian and African Studies* 7(1/2): 30–47.

Dyson-Hudson, R., and N. Dyson-Hudson

1980   "Nomadic Pastoralism." *Annual Review of Anthropology* 9: 15–61.

Edel, E.

1955   "Inschriften des alten Reiches. V. Die Reiseberichte des *Hrw-hwjf* (Herchuf)." *Ägyptologische Studien, Inst. für Orientforschung* 29: 51.

Ehgartner, W., and J. Jungwirth

1966   "Anthropologische Angaben über die Skelette der C-Gruppen- und Pan-Gräber aus dem Bezirk Sayala, Ägyptisch-Nubien." In M. Bietak, *Ausgrabungen in Sayala-Nubien 1961–1965: Denkmäler der C-Gruppe und der Pan-Gräber-Kultur*. Österreichische Akademie der Wissenschaften, Philosophisch-historische Klasse, Denkschriften 92. Vienna: Herman Böhlaus Nachf., 83–88.

Ekvall, R.B.

1961   "The Nomadic Pattern of Living Among Tibetans as Preparation for War." *American Anthropologist* 63: 1250–1263.

Elamin, Y., and A.M. Khabir
1987   "Neolithic Pottery from Survey Sites Around Shaqadud Cave, Western Butana, Sudan." *Archéologie du Nil Moyen* 2: 175–185.

Emery, W.B.
1938   *The Royal Tombs of Ballana and Qustol.* Service des Antiquités de l'Egypte. Mission Archéologique de Nubie 1929–1934. Cairo.

1965   *Egypt in Nubia.* London: Hutchinson.

Emery, W.B., and L.P. Kirwan
1935   *The Excavations and Survey Between Wadi es-Sebua and Adindan, 1929–1931.* Service des Antiquités de l'Egypte. Mission Archéologique de Nubie 1929–1934. Cairo.

Estigarribia, J.V.
1982   "Some Notes on Elephants and Meroe." *Meroitica* 6: 282–284. Berlin: Akademie Verlag.

Evans-Pritchard, E.E.
1927   "A Preliminary Account of the Ingessana Tribe in Fung Province." *Sudan Notes and Records* 10: 69–85.

1940   *The Nuer.* London: Oxford University Press.

Fairservice, W.A.
1972   "Preliminary Report on the first Two Seasons at Hierakonpolis." *Journal of the American Research Center, Egypt* 9: 7–27, 67–99.

Fattovich, R.
1972   "Yeha 1972: sondaggi stratigrafici." *Travaux R.C.P. 230, CNRS* 3: 65–75.

1979   "Trends in the Study of Predynastic Social Structure." *First International Congress of Egyptology, Cairo 1976, Actes.* Berlin, 215–220.

1984   "Remarks on the Dynamics of State Formation in Ancient Egypt." In Walter Dostal, ed., *On Social Evolution; Contributions to Anthropological Concepts. Vienna Contributions to Ethnology and Anthropology,* Vol. 1. Vienna: Verlag Ferdinand Berger & Söhne, 29–78.

1984a   "The Gash Delta Between 1000 BC and 1000 AD: An Archaeological Contribution to the Ancient History of the Eastern Sudan." Paper read at the Fifth International Conference for Meroitic Studies, Rome.

1984b   "The Late Prehistory of the Gash Delta." Paper read at the

International Symposium on the Late Prehistory of the Nile Basin and the Sahara, Poznan.

1984c   "Gash Delta Archaeological Project: 1980–1984 Field Seasons." Interim report of activity submitted to the Sudan Antiquities Service, Khartoum.

1984d   "Remarks on the Late Prehistory and Early History of Northern Ethiopia." *Proceedings of the 8th International Conference of Ethiopian Studies*. Addis Ababa.

1985   "The Problem of Punt in Light of Recent Field Work in the Eastern Sudan." Paper read at the Fourth International Congress of Egyptology, Munich.

1987   "Remarks on the Peopling of the Northern Ethiopian-Sudanese Borderland in Ancient Historical Times." In Loretta Del Francia, ed., *Studi in onore dui Ugo Monneret de Villard*, part I. *La valle del Nilo in epoca cristiana. Rivista degli Studi Orientali* 58 (Fasc. 1–4). Rome: Bardi Editore, 85–106.

1989   "The Stelae of Kassala: a New Type of Funerary Monuments in the Eastern Sudan." *Archéologie du Nil Moyen* 3: 55–71.

Fattovich, R., A.E. Marks, and A. Mohammed-Ali

1984   "The Archaeology of the Eastern Sahel, Sudan; Preliminary Results." *The African Archaeological Review* 2: 173–188.

Fattovich, R., K. Sadr, and S. Vitagliano

1988   "Societa e territorio nel delta del Gash (Kassala, Sudan orientale) 3000 a. Cr.–300/400 d. Cr." *Africa* 43 (3): 1–60.

Fattovich, R., and S. Vitagliano

1989   "Radiocarbon Dates from Mahal Teglinos, Kassala." *Nyame Akuma* 31: 39–40.

Firth, C.M.

1912   *The Archaeological Survey of Nubia, Report for 1908–1909* (2 volumes). Cairo: Government Press.

1915   *The Archaeological Survey of Nubia, Report for 1909–1910*. Cairo: Government Press.

1927   *The Archaeological Survey of Nubia, Report for 1910–1911*. Cairo: Government Press.

Flor, F.

1930   "Haustiere und Hirtenkulturen Kulturgeschichtliche Entwicklungsumrisse." *Wiener Beitrag zur Kulturgeschichte und Linguistik* 1: 1–238.

Galaty, J.G., D. Aronson, P.C. Salzman, and A. Chouinard (eds.)

1981   *The Future of Pastoral Peoples*. The International Development Research Center.

Galvin, K.F.

1987   "Forms of Finance and Forms of Production: The Evolution of Specialized Livestock Production in the Ancient Near East." In E.M. Brumfiel and T.K. Earle, eds., *Specialization, Exchange, and Complex Societies*. Cambridge: Cambridge University Press, 119–130.

Gamst, F.C.

1969   *The Qemant: A Pagan-Hebraic Peasantry of Ethiopia. Case Studies in Cultural Anthropology*. New York: Holt, Rinehart and Winston.

Garstang, J.

1903   *Mahasna and Bet-Khallaf*. London.

1911   *Meroe—The City of the Ethiopians*. Oxford.

Gasse, F., P. Rognon, and F.A. Street

1980   "Quaternary History of the Afar and Ethiopian Rift Lakes." In Williams and Faure, eds. (1980), *The Sahara and the Nile*, 361–400.

Gautier, A.

1986   "La faune de l'occupation néolithique d'el Kadada (secteurs 12-22-32) au Soudan central." *Archéologie du Nil Moyen* 1: 59–113.

Geddes, D.S.

1983   "Neolithic Transhumance in the Mediterranean Pyrenees." *World Archaeology* 15(1): 51–66.

Gellner, E.

1984   "Foreword." In A.M. Khazanov, ed., *Nomads and the Outside World*. Cambridge: Cambridge University Press.

Geraads, D.

1983   "Faunal Remains from the Gash Delta." *Nyame Akuma* 23: 22–23.

Geus, F.

1976   *Rapport annuel d'activité 1975–1976*. Khartoum: Sudan Antiquities Service, French Archaeological Research Unit.

1977   *Rapport annuel d'activité 1976–1977*. Khartoum: Sudan Antiquities Service, French Archaeological Research Unit.

1979   *Rapport annuel d'activité 1978–1979*. Khartoum: Sudan Antiquities Service, French Archaeological Research Unit.

1980   *Rapport annuel d'activité 1979–1980.* Khartoum: Directorate General for Antiquities and National Museums of the Sudan, French Archaeological Research Unit.

1982   *Rapport annuel d'activité 1980–1982.* Khartoum: Directorate General for Antiquities and National Museums of the Sudan, French Archaeological Research Unit.

1986   "La section française de la direction des antiquités du Soudan, Travaux de terrain et de laboratoire en 1982–1983." *Archéologie du Nil Moyen* 1: 13–59.

Gifford, D.P.

1978   "Ethnoarchaeological Observations of Natural Processes Affecting Cultural Materials." In R.A. Gould, ed., *Explorations in Ethnoarchaeology.* Albuquerque: University of New Mexico Press, 77–102.

1981   "Taphonomy and Paleoecology: A Critical Review of Archaeology's Sister Discipline." In M.B. Schiffer, ed., *Advances in Archaeological Method and Theory,* Vol. 4. New York: Academic Press, 365–438.

Gifford, D.P., G.L. Isaac, and C.M. Nelson

1980   "Evidence of Predation and Pastoralism at Prolonged Drift: A Pastoral Neolithic Site in Kenya." *Azania* 15: 7–108.

Gilbert, A.S.

1983   "On the Origins of Specialised Nomadic Pastoralism in Western Iran." *World Archaeology* 15(1): 105–119.

Goldschmidt, W.

1979   "A General Model for Pastoral Social Systems." In *Pastoral Production and Society* (1979), 15–29.

Gratien, B.

1978   *Les cultures Kerma: Essai de classification.* Lille: Lille University III Press.

Greene, D.L.

1967   *Dentition of Meroitic, X-Group and Christian Populations from Wadi Halfa, Sudan.* Anthropological Papers, University of Utah. Salt Lake City.

Greene, D.L., and G.J. Armelagos

1972   *The Wadi Halfa Mesolithic population.* Research Report No. 11, Department of Anthropology, University of Massachusetts. Amherst.

Griffith, F.L.

1924   "Oxford Excavations in Nubia." *University of Liverpool Annals of Archaeology and Anthropology* 11: 115–178.

Haaland, R.

1981   *Migratory Herdsmen and Cultivating Women: The Structure of Neolithic Seasonal Adaptation in the Khartoum Nile Environment.* Bergen.

1986   "Problems in the Mesolithic and Neolithic Culture History in the Central Nile Valley, Sudan." *Sixth International Conference for Nubian Studies, Prepublication of Main Papers,* Vol. 1. Klassik Institutt, University of Bergen.

1987   *Socio-Economic Differentiation in the Neolithic Sudan.* British Archaeological Reports International Series 350.

Hahn, J.

1988   "Settlement Patterns in the Gebel Kamil Area. Southwest Egypt." Paper delivered at the International Symposium on "Environmental Change and Human Culture in the Nile Basin and Northeast Africa Through the 2nd Millennium B.C." Dymaczewo, Poznan, 5–10 September 1988.

Hassan, F.A.

1984   "Environment and Subsistence in Predynastic Egypt." In J.D. Clark and S. A. Brandt, eds., *From Hunters to Farmers: The Causes and Consequences of Food Production in Africa.* Berkeley: University of California Press, 57–65.

1985   "Radiocarbon Chronology of Neolithic and Predynastic Sites in Upper Egypt and the Delta." *The African Archaeological Review* 3: 95–117.

Hays, T. R.

1971a   "The Karamakol Industry: Part of the 'Khartoum Horizon Style.'" In Shiner, ed. (1971a), *The Prehistory and Geology of Northern Sudan,* Part 1, 84–154.

1971b   "The Tergis Industry." In Shiner, ed. (1971a), *The Prehistory and Geology of Northern Sudan,* Part 1, 154–187.

1976   "Predynastic Egypt: Recent Field Research." *Current Anthropology* 17: 552–554.

Hesse, B.

1982   "Slaughter Patterns and Domestication: The Beginnings of Pastoralism in Western Iran." *Man,* New Series 17: 403–417.

1984 "These Are Our Goats: The Origins of Herding in West Central Iran." In J. Clutton-Brock and C. Grigson, eds., *Animals and Archaeology*, Vol. 3, *Early Herders and Their Flocks*. British Archaeological Reports, International Series, 202, 243–264.

Hintze, F.
1959 "Preliminary Report of the Butana Expedition, 1958." *Kush* 7: 171–197.

1967 "Meroe und die Noba." *Zeitschrift für ägyptische Sprache und Altertumskunde* 94: 79–86.

Hodder, I.
1982 *Symbols in Action: Ethnoarchaeological Studies of Material Culture*. Cambridge: Cambridge University Press.

Hofman, J.L.
1982 "Exploring Intrasite Patterning and Assemblage Variation on Historic Sheepherder Camp." *North American Archaeologist* 3(2): 89–111.

Hoffman, M.A.
1982 *The Predynastic of Hierakonpolis, an Interim Report*. Egyptian Studies Association, Publication No. 1. Oxford: Alden Press.

Hoffman, M.A., H.A. Hamroush, and R.O. Allen
1986 "A Model of Urban Development for the Hierakonpolis Region from Predynastic Through Old Kingdom Times." *Journal of the American Research Center in Egypt* 23: 175–187.

Hofmann, I.
1967 *Die Kulturen des Niltals von Aswan bis Sennar vom Mesolithikum bis zum Ende der Christlichen Epoche*. Monographien zur Völkerkunde, IV. Hamburg: Museum für Völkerkunde,.

Hole, F.D.
1974 "Tepe Tula'i: An Early Campsite in Khuzistan, Iran." *Paleorient* 2: 219–242.

1978 "Pastoral Nomadism in Western Iran." In R. Gould, ed., *Explorations in Ethnoarchaeology*. Albuquerque: University of New Mexico Press, 127–179.

1980 "The Prehistory of Herding: Some Suggestions from Ethnography." In *L'archéologie de l'Iraq du début de l'époque néolithique à 333 avant notre ère: perspectives et limites de l'interprétation anthropologique des documents*. Colloques internationaux du Centre National de la Recherche Scientifique, No. 580. Paris, 119–131.

Hole, F., and K.V. Flannery
 1967   "The Prehistory of Southwestern Iran: A Preliminary Report."
         Proceedings of the Prehistoric Society 33: 147–206.
Hole, F., K.V. Flannery, and J.A. Neely
 1969   *Prehistory and Human Ecology of the Dehluran Plain; An Early
         Village Sequence from Khuzistan, Iran*. Ann Arbor: University of
         Michigan Press.
Holy, L.
 1974   *Neighbours and Kinsmen: A Study of the Berti People of Darfur*.
         New York: St. Martin's Press.
Ibn Khaldun
 1396   *The Muqaddimah*. Translated by Franz Rosenthal. London:
 [1958] Routledge and Kegan Paul.
Irons, W.
 1968   "The Turkmen Nomads." *Natural History* (Nov.): 44–51.
 1979   "Political Stratification Among Pastoral Nomads." In *Pastoral
         Production and Society* (1979), 361–374.
Jackson, H.C.
 1923   "The Nuer of the Upper Nile Province." *Sudan Notes and Rec-
         ords* 6: 59–107, and 123–189.
Jacobs, A.H.
 1975   "African Pastoralists: Some General Remarks." *Anthropological
         Quarterly* 38(3): 144–154.
Jäkel,D.
 1978   "Eine Klimakurve für die Zentralsahara." In *Sahara, 10.000 Jahre
         zwischen Weide und Wüste*. Museen Köln, 382–396.
James, W.
 1979   *Kwanim Pa: The Making of the Uduk People*. Oxford: Clarendon
         Press.
Johnson, D.L.
 1969   *The Nature of Nomadism: A Comparative Study of Pastoral Migra-
         tions in Southwestern Asia and Northern Africa*. University of
         Chicago, Department of Geography Research Paper, No. 118.
         Chicago.
Johnson, G.A.
 1981   "Monitoring Complex System Integration and Boundary Phe-
         nomena with Settlement Size Data." In S.E. van der Leeuw, ed.,
         Archaeological Approaches to the Study of Complexity. Amsterdam:
         Amsterdam University Press, 144–190.

Kaiser, W.

1961   "Bericht über eine archäologische-geologische Felduntersuch-
ung in Ober- und Mittelägypten." *Mitteilungen des deutschen
archäologischen Institut, Abteilung Kairo* 17: 1–53.

Kantor, H.J.

1944   "The Final Phase of the Predynastic Culture: Gerzean or Semainean." *Journal of Near Eastern Studies* 3: 110–136.

1965   "The Relative Chronology of Egypt and Its Foreign Correla-
tions Before the Late Bronze Age." In R.W. Ehrich, ed., *Chronologies in Old World Archaeology*. Chicago: University of Chicago Press, 1–46.

Khazanov, A.M.

1984   *Nomads and the Outside World*. Cambridge: Cambridge University Press.

Kirwan, L.P.

1958   "Comments on the Origins and History of the Nobatae of
Procopius." *Kush* 6: 69–74.

1972a   "The Christian Topography and the Kingdom of Axum." *The
Geographical Journal* 138(2): 166–178.

1972b   "An Ethiopian-Sudanese Frontier Zone in Ancient History."
The Geographical Journal 138(4): 457–466.

1974   "Nubia and Nubian Origins." *The Geographical Journal* 140(1):
43–52.

1978   "Beyond Roman Egypt's Desert Frontiers." *The Geographical
Journal* 144(2): 294–297.

1982   "The X-Group Problem." *Meroitica* 6:191–205.

Kitchen, K.A.

1982   "Punt." *Lexikon der Ägyptologie* (IV, 8) 32: 1198–1201.

Klein, J.

1920   "The Mesta: A Study of Spanish Economic History." *Harvard
Economic Studies* 21:1273–1836.

Klein, R.G., and K. Cruz-Uribe

1984   *The Analysis of Animal Bones from Archaeological Sites*. Chicago:
University of Chicago Press.

Kobishchanov, Y. M. (ed.)

1979   *Axum*. University Park: Pennsylvania State University Press.

Krader, L.

1959   "The Ecology of Nomadic Pastoralism." *International Social
Science Journal* 11(4): 499–510.

Kroeber, A.L.

1948   *Anthropology*. New York: Harcourt Brace.

Krzyzaniak, L.

1977a   *Early Farming Cultures on the Lower Nile*. Warsaw.

1977b   "New Light on Early Food Production in the Central Sudan." *Journal of African History* 19(2): 159–172.

Kuper, R.

1981   "Untersuchungen zur Besiedlungsgeschichte der östlichen Sahara." *Beiträge zur Allgemeine und Vergleichende Archäologie* 3: 215–175.

1986   "Wadi Howar and Laqiya; Recent Field Studies into the Early Settlement of Northern Sudan." In M. Krause, ed., *Nubische Studien*. Mainz a. R.: Ph. von Zabern.

1988   "When Sudan Was in Egypt's Land." Paper delivered at the International Symposium on "Environmental Change and Human Culture in the Nile Basin and Northeast Africa Through the 2nd Millennium B.C." Dymaczewo, Poznan, 5–10 September 1988.

Lal, B.B.

1967   "Indian Archaeological Expedition to Nubia, 1962. A Preliminary Report." *Fouilles en Nubie (1961–1963)*. Cairo: Service des Antiquités de l'Egypte, 97–118.

Lattimore, O.

1967   *Inner Asian Frontiers of China*. Boston: Beacon Press.

Launer, H.M.

1981   "Ideology, Kinship and Cognatic Descent Among the Gaam (Ingessana) of Eastern Sudan." In M.L. Bender, ed., *Peoples and Cultures of the Ethio-Sudan Borderlands*. Committee on Northeast African Studies, African Studies Center, Monograph no. 10. Ann Arbor: University of Michigan, 61–79.

Leclant, J.

1959   "Haoulti-Melazo (1955–1956)." *Annales d'Éthiopie* 3:43–82.

Lee, R.B., and I. DeVore

1968   "Problems in the Study of Hunters and Gatherers." In R.B. Lee and I. DeVore, eds., *Man the Hunter*. Chicago: Aldine, 3–12.

Lees, S.H., and D.G. Bates

1974   "The Origins of Specialized Pastoralism: A Systemic Model." *American Antiquity* 39(2/1): 187–193.

Lefébure, C.
1979   "Introduction: the Specificity of Nomadic Pastoral Societies."
        In *Pastoral Production and Society* (1979), 1–15.

Lenoble, P.
1987   "Quatre tumulus sur mille du Djebel Makbor A.M.S. NE-36-0 /
        3-x-1." *Archéologie du Nil Moyen* 2: 207–248.

1987a   "Trois tombes de la région de Meroe, la cloture des fouilles
        historiques d' el Kadada en 1985 et 1986." *Archéologie du Nil
        Moyen* 2: 89–121.

Levy, T.E.
1983   "The Emergence of Specialised Pastoralism in the Southern
        Levant." *World Archaeology* 15(1): 15–37.

Lewis, B.A.
1972   *The Murle: Red Chiefs and Black Commoners.* Oxford: Claren-
        don Press.

Littman, E.
1913   *Reisebericht der Expedition/Topographie und Geschichte Aksums,
        Deutsche Aksum Expedition,* vol. I. Berlin: Georg Reimer.

Livingstone, D.A.
1980   "Environmental Changes in the Nile Headwaters." In Williams
        and Faure, eds., *The Sahara and the Nile.* 339–359.

Lloyd, A.B.
1983   "The Late Period, 664–323 BC." In B.G. Trigger, B.J. Kemp, D.
        O'Connor, and A.B. Lloyd, *Ancient Egypt: A Social History.*
        Cambridge: Cambridge University Press, 279–349.

Logan, M.H.
1918   "The Beirs." *Sudan Notes and Records* 1: 238–249.

Lynch, T.F.
1983   "Camelid Pastoralism and the Emergence of Tiwanaku Civiliza-
        tion in the South-Central Andes." *World Archaeology* 15(1): 1–15.

MacIver, D.R., and C.L. Woolley
1909   *Areika.* Eckley B. Coxe Junior Expedition to Nubia, volume I.
        Philadelphia: University of Pennsylvania Press.

1911   *Buhen.* Eckley B. Coxe Junior Expedition to Nubia, volumes
        VII and VIII. Philadelphia: University of Pennsylvania Press.

Marks, A.E., A. Mohammed-Ali, and R. Fattovich
1986   "The Archaeology of the Eastern Sudan: A First Look." *Archae-
        ology* 39(5): 44–50.

Marks, A.E., and C.R. Ferring
1971   "The Karat Group: An Early Ceramic Bearing Occupation of the Dongola Reach, Sudan." In Shiner, ed. (1971a), *Prehistory and Geology of Northern Sudan*, Part 1, 187–276.

Marks, A.E., A. Mohammed-Ali, J. Peters, and R.Robertson
1985   "The Prehistory of the Central Nile Valley as seen from its Eastern Hinterlands: Excavations at Shaqadud, Sudan." *Journal of Field Archaeology* 12: 262–278.

Marks, A.E., and K. Sadr
1988   "Holocene Environments and Occupations in the Southern Atbai, Sudan: A Preliminary Formulation." In J.Bower and D. Lubell, eds., *Prehistoric Cultures and Environments in the Late Quaternary of Africa*. British Archaeological Reports International Series 405, 69–91.

Marx, E.
1978   "The Ecology and Politics of Nomadic Pastoralists in the Middle East." In W. Weissleder, ed., *The Nomadic Alternative. Modes and Models of Interaction in the African-Asian Deserts and Steppes*. The Hague: Mouton, 41–47.

Michels, J.W.
1979   "Axumite Archaeology: an Introductory Essay." In Kobishchanov, ed. (1979), *Axum*, 1–35.

Mills, A.J., and H-Å. Nordström
1966   "The Archaeological Survey from Gemai to Dal. Preliminary Report on the Season 1964–65." *Kush* 14: 1–15.

Mohammed-Ali, A.S.
1982   *The Neolithic Period in the Sudan, c. 6000–2500 BC*. Cambridge Monographs in African Archaeology, 6. British Archaeological Reports, International Series, 139.

Mond, Sir R., and O. H. Myers
1937   *Cemeteries of Armant*. 2 vols. London: The Egypt Exploration Society.

Monneret de Villard, U.
1938   *Storia della Nubia cristiana*. Rome.
1938a   "Aksum: Ricerche di topografia generale." *Analecta Orientale* 16: 1–138.

Monod, T. (ed.)
1975   *Pastoralism in Tropical Africa. Studies Presented and Discussed at*

the XIIIth International African Seminar, Niamey, 1972. London: Oxford University Press, Introduction, 99–183.

Murdock, G.P., and S.F. Wilson

1972 "Settlement Patterns and Community Organization: Cross-Cultural Codes 3." *Ethnology* 11(3): 254–295.

Murray, G.W.

1967 "Trogodytica: The Red Sea Littoral in Ptolemaic Times." *Geographical Journal* 133(1): 24–33.

Muzzolini, A.

1982 "Les climates sahariens durant l'Holocène et la fin du Pléistocène." *Travaux du Laboratoire d'Anthropologie, de Préhistoire, et d'Ethnologie des pays de la Méditerranée Occidentale* 2: 1–38.

Myers, O. H.

1958 "Abka Re-excavated." *Kush* 6: 131–141.

1960 "Abka Again." *Kush* 8: 174–181.

Nadel, S.F.

1945 "Notes on Beni Amer Society." *Sudan Notes and Records* 26: 51–95.

Neumann, K.

1989 "Holocene Vegetation of the Eastern Sahara: Charcoal from Prehistoric Sites." *The African Archaeological Review* 7: 97–117.

Nomadismus als Entwicklungsproblem.

1969 Bertelsmann Universitätsverlag.

Nordström, H.-Å.

1972 *Neolithic and A-Group sites. The Scandinavian Joint Expedition to Sudanese Nubia,* vol. 3. Uppsala.

O'Connor, D.

1986 "The Locations of Yam and Kush and Their Historical Implications." *Journal of the American Research Center in Egypt* 23: 27–51.

Otto, K.H.

1963 "Shaqadud." *Kush* 11: 108–115.

Owen, T.R.H.

1937 "The Hadendowa." *Sudan Notes and Records* 20(2): 183–208.

Oxenstierna, E.

1967 "The Vikings." *Scientific American,* May 1967.

Pachur, H.J.

1975 "Zur spätpleistozänen und holozänen Formung auf der Nordabdachung des Tibestigebirges." *Die Erde* 1–2: 25–46.

Pastoral Production and Society
1979 Proceedings of the International Meeting on Nomadic Pastoralism, Paris, 1–3 December 1976. Ed. by L'Équipe écologie et anthropologie des sociétés pastorales. Cambridge: Cambridge University Press.

Paul, A.
1954 *A History of the Beja Tribes of the Sudan*. Cambridge: Cambridge University Press.
1950 "Notes on the Beni Amer." *Sudan Notes and Records* 31: 223–246.

Payne, S.
1973 "Kill-off Patterns in Sheep and Goats: the Mandibles from Asvan Kale." *Anatolian Studies* 13: 281–303.

Peet, T. E.
1914 *The Cemeteries of Abydos*. Part 2. *1911–1912*. The Egypt Exploration Fund, Excavation Memoir, 34. London.

Peters, J.
1986 "Bijdrage tot de Archeozöologie van Soedan en Egypte." Ph.D. dissertation, Rijksuniversiteit Gent, Fakulteit der Wetenschappen.

Petit-Maire, N.
1979 "Cadre écologique et peuplement humain: le littoral Ouest-saharien depuis 10.000 ans." *L'Anthropologie* 83(1): 69–82.

Petrie, W.M.F.
1896 *Naqada and Ballas*. London: Quaritch.

Phillipson, D.W
1977 *The Later Prehistory of Eastern and Southern Africa*. New York: Africana.
1977a "The Excavation of Gobedra Rock-Shelter, Axum." *Azania* 12: 53–83.

Piotrovsky, B.
1967 "The Early Dynasty Settlement at Khor-Daoud and Wadi-Allaki: The Ancient Route to the Gold Mines." In *Fouilles en Nubie (1961–1963)*. Cairo: Service des Antiquités de l'Egypte, 127–140.

Privati, B.
1987 "Notes sur la céramique du tumulus 3 du Djebel Makbor." *Archéologie du Nil Moyen* 2: 248–249.
1988 "La céramique de l'établissement pre-Kerma." *Geneva* 36: 21–25

Puglisi, S.
1941   "Primi risultati delle indagini compiute dalla missione arch-
eologica di Aksum." *Africa Italiana* 8(3–4): 95–153.

Reed, C.A.
1959   "Animal Domestication in the Prehistoric Near East." *Science*
130(3383): 1629–1639.

Reisner, G.A.
1910   *The Archaeological Survey of Nubia, Report for 1907–1908.* Cairo:
National Printing Department.
1917   "The Barkal Temples in 1916." *Journal of Egyptian Archaeology* 4:
213–227.
1918   "Preliminary Report on the Harvard-Boston Excavations at
Nuri: The Kings of Ethiopia after Tirhaqa." *Harvard African
Studies* 2: 1–65.
1923   *Excavations at Kerma, I–III. Harvard African Studies* 5. Cambridge, Mass.

Reinold, J.
1987   "Les fouilles pre- et proto-historiques de la section française de
la direction des antiquités du Soudan: Les campagnes 1984–85
et '85–86." *Archéologie du Nil Moyen* 2: 17–61.

Richter, J.
1984   "Ceramic Sites in the Wadi Howar, Sudan." Paper presented at
the symposium on the Late Prehistory of the Nile Basin and the
Eastern Sahara, Poznan.

Rizkana, I., and J. Seeher
1985   "The Chipped Stones at Maadi: Preliminary Assessment of a
Predynastic Industry and its Long-Distance Relations." *Mitteilungen des Deutsches Archäologisches Institut Abteilung Kairo*
41: 235–255.

Robbins, L.H.
1973   "Turkana Material Culture Viewed from an Archaeological Perspective." *World Archaeology* 5(2): 209–214.

Robertshaw, P.T., and D.P. Collett
1983   "The Identification of Pastoral Peoples in the Archaeological
Record: An Example from East Africa." *World Archaeology* 15(1):
67–78.

Rosen, S.A.
1988   "Notes on the Origins of Pastoral Nomadism: A Case Study

from the Negev and Sinai." *Curent Anthropology* 29 (3): 498–506.

Sadr, K.

1983 "Interim Report on Late Prehistoric Settlement Patterns of the Khashm el Girba Area, East Central Sudan." *Nyame Akuma* 22: 28–30.

1986 "Preliminary Report on the Archaeological Settlement Patterns of the Kassala Area." *Annali del Istituto Universitario Orientale* 46(1): 1–34.

1987 "The Territorial Expanse of the Pan-Grave Culture." *Archéologie du Nil Moyen* 2: 265–293.

1990 "The Medjay in the Southern Atbai." *Archéologie du Nil Moyen* 4.

Saeed, E.M.

1969 *Ground Water Appraisal of the Gash River Basin at Kassala, Kassala Province. Democratic Republic of the Sudan,* Geological and Mineral Resources Department, Bulletin no. 17. Khartoum: Sudan Survey Department.

1972 *Hydrogeology of Kassala District, Kassala Province. Democratic Republic of the Sudan,* Geological and Mineral Resources Department, Bulletin no. 21. Khartoum: Sudan Survey Department.

Salzman, P.C.

1978 "The Proto-State in Iranian Baluchistan." In R. Cohen and E.R. Service, eds., *The Origins of the State.* Philadelphia: Institute for the Study of Human Issues, 125–141.

Sandars, G.E.R.

1933 "The Bisharin." *Sudan Notes and Records* 16: 119–151.

Sauer, C.O.

1952 *Agricultural Origins and Dispersals.* New York: American Geographical Society.

Sauneron, S.

1965 "Un village nubien fortifié sur la rive orientale de Ouadi es-Sébou." *Bulletin de l'Institut français d'archéologie orientale* 63(1965): 161–167.

Säve-Söderbergh, T.

1941 *Ägypten und Nubien: Ein Beitrag zur Geschichte altägyptischer Aussenpolitik.* Lund: Håkan Ohlssons Boktryckeri.

Schild, R., M. Chmielewska, and H. Wieckowska

1968　"The Arkinian and Shamarkian Industries." In Wendorf, ed. (1968), *The Prehistory of Nubia*, vol. 2, 651–768.

Schild, R., and F. Wendorf

1984　"Lithostratigraphy of Holocene Lakes Along the Kiseiba Scarp." In Wendorf, Schild, and Close (1984), *Cattle-Keepers of the Eastern Sahara*, 9–41.

Schmidt, W., and W. Koppers

1924　*Völker und Kulturen*. Part 1, *Gesellschaft und Wirtschaft der Völker*. Regensburg: Josef Habbel.

Schuck, W.

1988　"An Archaeological Survey in the Selima Sandsheet." Paper delivered at the International Symposium on "Environmental Change and Human Culture in the Nile Basin and Northeast Africa Through the 2nd Millennium B.C." Dymaczewo, Poznan, 5–10 September 1988.

Sealy, J.C., and N.J. van der Merwe

1987　"Stable Carbon Isotopes, Later Stone Age Diets and Seasonal Mobility in the Southwestern Cape." In J. Parkington and M. Hall, eds., *Papers in the Prehistory of the Western Cape, South Africa*. British Archaeological Reports International Series 332 (i&ii), 262–269.

Servant, M., and S. Servant-Vildary

1980　"L'environment quaternaire du bassin du Tchad." In Williams and Faure, eds. (1980), *The Sahara and the Nile*, 133–162.

Service, E.R.

1975　*Origins of the State and Civilization*. New York: Norton.

Sethe, K.

1906　"Urkunden der 18. Dynastie. Historisch-biographische Urkunden." In G. Steindorff, ed., *Urkunden des ägyptischen Altertums*. Leipzig.

1932　"Urkunden des Altes Reichs II." In G. Steindorff, ed., *Urkunden des ägyptischen Altertums*. Leipzig.

Shahrani, M.N.M.

1979　*The Kirghiz and Wakhi of Afghanistan: Adaptation to Closed Frontiers*. Seattle: University of Washington Press.

Sherratt, A.G.

1983　"The Secondary Exploitation of Animals in the Old World." *World Archaeology* 15(1): 3–26.

Shimada, M., and I. Shimada

1985   "Prehistoric Llama Breeding and Herding on the North Coast of Peru." *American Antiquity* 50(1): 3–26.

Shiner, J.L.

1968a   "The Khartoum Variant Industry." In Wendorf, ed. (1968), *The Prehistory of Nubia,* 768–791.

1968b   "The Cataract Tradition." In Wendorf, ed. (1968), *The Prehistory of Nubia,* 535–630.

1971a   (ed.) *The Prehistory and Geology of Northern Sudan,* 2 parts. Report to the National Science Foundation, Grant GS 1192.

1971b   "El Melik Group." In Shiner, ed. (1971a), 276–291.

Shinnie, P.L.

1967   *Meroe.* London: Thames and Hudson.

Simmons, A.H., I. Köhler-Rollefson, G.O.Rollefsaon, R. Mandel, and Z. Kafafi

1988   "Ain-Ghazal: A major Neolithic Settlement in Central Jordan." *Science* 240: 35–40.

Smith, A.B.

1976   "A Microlithic Industry from Adrar Bous, Teneré Desert, Niger." *Proceedings of the Seventh Panafrican Congress for Prehistory.* Addis Ababa, 181–196.

1980   "The Neolithic Tradition in the Sahara." In Williams and Faure, eds. (1980), *The Sahara and the Nile,* 451–467.

1984   "Origins of the Neolithic in the Sahara." In J.D. Clark and S.A. Brandt, eds., *From Hunters to Farmers: The Causes and Consequences of Food Production in Africa.* Berkeley: University of California Press, 84–93.

Smith, H.S.

1962   *Preliminary Reports of the Egypt Exploration Society's Nubian Survey.* Cairo.

Smith, P., and L.K. Horowitz

1984   "Radiographic Evidence for Changing Patterns of Animal Exploitation in the Southern Levant." *Journal of Archaeological Science* 11: 467–475.

Smith, S.E.

1980   "The Environmental Adaptation of Nomads in the West African Sahel: A Key to Understanding Prehistoric Pastoralists." In Williams and Faure, eds. (1980), *The Sahara and the Nile,* 467–489.

Smither, P.C.

1945　"The Semnah Despatches." *Journal of Egyptian Archaeology* 31: 3–10.

Spooner, B.

1972　"The Status of Nomadism as a Cultural Phenomenon in the Middle East." *Journal of Asian and African Studies* 7(1/2): 122–131.

1973　*The Cultural Ecology of Pastoral Nomads.* Addison-Wesley Module in Anthropology, no. 45. Reading, Mass.: Addison-Wesley.

Steindorff, G.

1937　*Aniba. Mission Archéologique de Nubie 1929–1934,* vol. 1. Hamburg: Glückstadt.

Swift, J.

1979　"The Development of Livestock Trading in Nomad Pastoral Economy: The Somali Case." In *Pastoral Production and Society* (1979), 447–467.

Talbot, M.R.

1980　"Environmental Responses to Climatic Change in the West African Sahel over the Past 20,000 Years." In Williams and Faure, eds. (1980), *The Sahara and the Nile,* 37–62.

Taylor, W.W.

1972　"The Hunter-Gatherer Nomads of Northern Mexico: A Comparison of the Archival and Archaeological Records." *World Archaeology* 4(2): 167–179.

Thurnwald, R.

1932　*Economics in Primitive Communities.* London: Oxford University Press.

Tornay, S.

1981　"The Nyangatom: an Outline of Their Ecology and Social Organization." In M.L. Bender, ed., *Peoples and Cultures of the Ethio-Sudan Borderlands. Committee on Northeast African Studies.* Monograph no. 10. Michigan State University: African Studies Center, 137–179.

Trigger, B.G.

1965　*History and Settlement in Lower Nubia. Yale University Publications in Anthropology,* no. 69. New Haven, Conn.

1967　*The Late Nubian Settlement at Arminna West.* Publications of the Pennsylvania-Yale Expedition to Egypt, no. 2. New Haven, Conn., and Philadelphia.

1969   "The Royal Tombs at Qustul and Ballana and their Meroitic Antecedents." *Journal of Egyptian Archaeology* 55: 117–128.

1976   *Nubia Under the Pharaohs.* London: Thames and Hudson.

van den Brink, E. C. M. (ed.)

1988   *The Archaeology of the Nile Delta: Problems and Priorities.* Amsterdam: Netherlands Foundation for Archaeological Research in Egypt.

Vercoutter, J.

1958   "Excavations in Sai, 1955–57." *Kush* 6: 144–169.

Veyret, P.

1951   *Géographie de l'élevage.* Paris: Libraire Gallimard.

Vignard, E.

1920   "Station Aurignacenne à Nag "Hamdi." *Bulletin de l'Institut français d'Archéologie Orientale* 18: 1–20.

Vila, A.

1975–   *La prospection archéologique de la Vallée du Nil, au sud de la*
1984   *Cataracte de Dal (Nubie Soudanaise),* 14 Fascicules. Paris: Centre National des Recherches Scientifiques.

Warren, A.

1970   "Dune Trends and their Implications in the Central Sudan." *Zeitschrift Geomorphologie, NF,* Supplement 10: 154–180.

Weigall, A.E.P.

1907   *A Report on the Antiquities of Lower Nubia and their Condition in 1906–7.* Oxford.

Weissleder, W. (ed.)

1978   *The Nomadic Alternative. Modes and Models of Interaction in the African-Asian Deserts and Steppes.* The Hague: Mouton.

Wendorf, F. (ed.)

1968   *The Prehistory of Nubia.* 2 vols. Dallas, Tex.: Southern Methodist University Press

Wendorf, F., and R. Schild (eds.)

1980   *Prehistory of the Eastern Sahara.* New York, Academic Press.

Wendorf, F., R. Schild, and A.E. Close (assemblers and editor)

1984   *Cattle-Keepers of the Eastern Sahara: The Neolithic of Bir Kiseiba.* New Delhi: Pauls Press.

Wenke, R.J.

1989   "Egypt: Origins of Complex Societies." *Annual Review of Anthropology* 18: 129–155.

Wickens, G.E.

1982   "Paleobotanical Speculations and Quaternary Environments in the Sudan." In M.A.J. Williams and D.A. Adamson, eds., *A Land Between Two Niles: Quaternary Geology and Biology of the Central Sudan*. Rotterdam: A.A. Balkema, 23–51.

Wilkinson, P.F.

1976   "Random Hunting and the Composition of Faunal Samples from Archaeological Excavations: A Modern Example from New Zealand." *Journal of Archaeological Science* 3: 321–328.

Williams, M.A.J., and H. Faure (eds.)

1980   *The Sahara and the Nile: Quaternary Environments and Prehistoric Occupation in Northern Africa*. Rotterdam: A.A. Balkema.

Wilson, J.A.

1951   *The Culture of Ancient Egypt*. Chicago: University of Chicago Press.

Wright, H.T., and G.A. Johnson

1975   "Population, Exchange and Early State Formation in Southwestern Iran." *American Anthropologist* 77: 267–289.

Zagarell, A.

1983   "Prehistory of the Northern Bahtiyari Mountains." *Tübinger Atlas*, series B 42: 1–87.

Index

This book has been set in Linotron Galliard. Galliard was designed for Mergenthaler in 1978 by Matthew Carter. Galliard retains many of the features of a sixteenth century typeface cut by Robert Granjon but has some modifications which gives it a more contemporary look.

Printed on acid-free paper.